A New Ostpolitik –
Strategies for a United Europe

A New Ostpolitik – Strategies for a United Europe

Werner Weidenfeld (ed.)

Eric von Breska
Petra Brunner
Martin Brusis
Josef Janning
Barbara von Ow

Strategies for Europe

Bertelsmann Foundation Publishers
Gütersloh 1997

Die Deutsche Bibliothek – CIP-Einheitsaufnahme
A New Ostpolitik - Strategies for a United Europe / Werner
Weidenfeld (ed.). Eric von Breska ... [Transl.: Gabriele Schroers]. -
Gütersloh : Bertelsmann Foundation, Publ., 1997
  Dt. Ausg. u. d. T.: Neue Ostpolitik - Strategie für eine
gesamteuropäische Entwicklung
  ISBN 3 - 89204 - 816 - 9

© 1997 Bertelsmann Foundation Publishers, Gütersloh
Responsible: Cornelius Ochmann
Editor: Eric von Breska
Translation: Gabriele Schroers
Copy editor: Brigitte Neuparth
Production editor: Kerstin Stoll
Cover design: HTG Werbeagentur, Bielefeld
Cover photo: The Image Bank, Pierre-Yves Goavec
Typesetting: Jung Satzcentrum, Lahnau
Print: Fuldaer Verlagsanstalt GmbH
ISBN 3-89204-816-9

Table of Contents

Summary 9

Preface 17

I. Situation 19

    1. Central and Eastern Europe 19
    2. The Balkans 26
    3. Russia and the CIS 32

II. Risks 37

    1. Central and Eastern Europe 37

        Stagnating modernisation and social conflicts 37
        Environmental problems 39
        Growing crime rate 41
        Lacking reform capacity of the EU 42
        Unsolved security questions 45

    2. The Balkans 47

        Precarious peace in Bosnia 47
        Security risks of a disintegration of Bosnia 49
        Potential conflicts in the southern Balkans 51
        Underdevelopment and political destabilisation 54

    3. Russia and the CIS 57

        Disintegration or reintegration 57
        Slow democratisation 60
        Economic setbacks 63
        Russia as unpredictable super-power 67
        Nuclear and ecological time bombs 70

III. Aims of the EU *Ostpolitik* 73

    1. Central and Eastern Europe: integration into the EU 73
    2. The Balkans: stabilising peace 76
    3. Russia and the CIS: cooperation and
        "strategic partnership" 79

IV. Strategies of a new *Ostpolitik* 83

    1. Central and Eastern Europe: strategy for enlargement 83

        Efforts to be made by the associated states 84
        Internal reforms of the EU and balance of interests 87
        Structuring the integration process 90
        Further development of the EU within the framework
        of differentiated integration 93
        A differentiated concept for European security 97

    2. The Balkans: stabilising peace 100

        Linking border guarantees and renunciation-of-violence
        guarantees 101
        Flexible and graded cooperation 103
        Coping with minority problems 106
        Economic development 110
        Strengthening civil society 112

3. Russia and the CIS: partnership and cooperation......... 114

    Aiding democracy and freedom of the media 116
    Investment and the opening of markets 119
    Integration and cooperation in the new Europe 122
    The West and the other CIS member states 126
    Programme for nuclear and ecological redevelopment 130

V. Overcoming the new borders......................... 133

    1. Strengthening the OSCE and the Council of Europe...... 134
    2. Developing regional cooperation 137
    3. Promoting cooperation between border regions.......... 141
    4. Networking Europe 144

Appendix

    Tables 147
    Bibliography....................................... 151
    The authors.. 163
    The project partners 169
    The publications 171

Summary

Seven years after the historic change of 1989, the future of Europe as a whole is still uncertain. Diverging transformation processes are dividing the east of Europe into new political and economic sectors. While the transformation of systems is quickly progressing in the ten Central and Eastern European states associated with the European Union (EU), the development in the Balkan countries as well as Russia and the CIS is further falling behind. In terms of developing new concepts, the western states reacted much more passively to the radical changes in Eastern Europe than they had done in the post-war and reconstruction period in Western Europe. To date, individual interests and short-sighted adherence to vested rights superimpose the development of political priorities and ensuing coordinated programmes.

The great aim of European *Ostpolitik*, all-European integration under the shelter of the European Union, is endangered. The countries of Western Europe are the only countries with the necessary resources to stabilise the old Continent; to be involved within its framework is the target of most reform states. Europe is in need of a political concept towards Eastern Europe which permits to direct transformation and take the edge off inevitable dividing lines. In Central and Eastern Europe the focus is to be placed on EU enlargement; stabilising peace is of major importance in the Balkans; partnership and cooperation are at the centre of relations vis-à-vis Russia and the CIS. All three approaches must be complemented by an overall concept of transnational neighbourhood, which balances conflicts and tensions evolving from these differences in integrational denseness.

Strategy of eastern enlargement

Even though the associated states of Central and Eastern Europe (CEE states) have made considerable progress on the way towards democracy and market economy, the lasting success of transformation is not secure. Growing social inequality and unemployment strenghten populist forces. The earnings gap between east and west provides further incentives for migration into the EU. If environmental protection in Central and Eastern Europe continues to be neglected, cross-border emission, ecological damage and redevelopment costs can assume alarming proportions for the west. The spread of criminal structures discredits the new democratic institutions established under the rule of law and fuels the fear of eastern enlargement in the EU member states.

Meanwhile, the greatest obstacle to an eastern enlargement of the EU is no longer the state of development of the CEE states, but the lacking reform capacity of the European Union. Without a fundamental reform of institutions as well as structural and agricultural policy, incapacitation and insolvency of an enlarged Union are imminent. Without a compromise between the present member states, eastern enlargement will fail because of intensified distribution conflicts within the Community.

Four components must be linked in order to render the enlargement strategy successful: the Central and Eastern European countries' willingness to adjust further to the EU; the Union's political will to create the preconditions for an eastern enlargement by internal reforms and internal accommodation of conflicting interests; structuring the process of integration in clearly scheduled stages as well as the EU's further development in accordance with the model of differentiated integration.

The states associated with the EU can guarantee the success of eastern enlargement by pushing the application of the acquis communautaire of the EU beyond the basic criteria of the Copenhagen Summit, by avoiding special national demands and by definitely settling intraregional conflicts before joining the EU. More efficient decision-making processes are required in order to secure the efficiency of the EU. The necessary reforms include the extension of majority decisions in the Council of Ministers and the strengthening of the political leadership by modernising the presidency, reducing the Commission in size and consolidating the European Parliament. The Common Agricultural Policy must be re-oriented towards the market, and financial means from the structural funds must be geographically and thematically concentrated.

The core of European *Ostpolitik* will be the way in which accession is negotiated. The process should be oriented towards the "starting line model", instead of starting with talks with a special group of candidates ("group model"). A simultaneous start of negotiations with all associated states allows for a sliding transition into the integration process, prevents dissociation of successful reform states, such as Estonia and Slovenia, and keeps up pressure on political reforms vis-à-vis Slovakia. As for its impact, the starting line model would correspond to the "European Conference" suggested by France. Within its framework further approximation of the CEE states could be coordinated, their access to the market could be improved, and forms of political participation of those states which will only later become capable of joining the EU could be developed.

With eastern enlargement the European Union will need a new concept to define its self-image and its future role and structure. The future progress of integration cannot be guaranteed by a directed sequence of deepening and enlarging steps. In order to enable the Internal Market to extend undividedly, differentiation of the EU is required. It is concentrated on two clearly defined policy fields with substantial prerequisites for entry, whose institutional structure can have a very simple design in view of the convergence conditions: economic and monetary union and defence union, which is to be established. Differentiation of integration will keep the large EU governable by offering its efficient member states incentives for integrating their resources.

European peace policy in the Balkans

The Dayton Peace Accords constructed an extremely fragile state in Bosnia-Herzegovina, whose stability is solely based on the presence of the SFOR (Stabilisation Force) troops. There are clear indications that after the withdrawal of the troops Serb and Croat minorities and their respective patron states will form coalitions of interest, which aim at a secession of the Serb republic or the Croat cantons respectively. Its consequences would render the military involvement of the West worthless. In the southern part of the Balkans different parties have been opposing each other for years. If, in addition, the situation escalated into an armed conflict between ethnic Albanians in Kosovo and the Federal Republic of Yugoslavia, this would also fundamentally shake the young Macedonian state, and in the worst case even involve the neighbour states in the confrontation. European *Ostpolitik* therefore needs a strategy for peace for the Balkans which eliminates the causes of violent escalation of ethnic conflicts. With this aim in view structures for cooperation and negotiation must be organised, and the development of the Balkan countries must be promoted with regard to civil society and economy.

In order to stabilise the situation, such a strategy must be based on safe borders. To prevent governments from abusing state sovereignty for oppressing and discriminating against minorities and representatives of the opposition, all political actors must renounce the use of force in settling their conflicts. A legal basis which enables neutral parties to interfere is needed; in contrast to the traditonal position of the UN, this legal basis would also refer to the use of violence within states if it constituted a severe offence against human rights. Legitimation by multilateral organisations will still be required. It will be necessary to determine under which circumstances international military presence can be continued as long as there is a risk that the parties involved might again resort to violence when pursuing their interests. A more realistic strategy should maintain the unity of the state of Bosnia-Herzegovina, but accept the de facto separation into Bosnian-Muslim, Serb and Croat settlement areas.

The EU needs regulations which make different stages of political and economic cooperation with the Balkan states subject to clear-cut conditions. These regulations should become binding for EU member states, i. e. be formulated as Common Action within the framework of Common Foreign and Security Policy (CFSP). Beyond trade and cooperation agreements the Balkan countries are in need of a clear perspective of EU association and later EU membership, which will be combined with normative preconditions and specific programmes for the development of democracy. In addition to regional cooperation, politico-administrative decentralisation and regionalisation of these countries ought to be made a prerequisite of cooperation with the EU. Along the lines of the Stability Pact in Europe, the EU should initiate the conclusion of bilateral basic treaties – e. g. between Albania and the Federal Republic of Yugoslavia (FRY) and Macedonia. Vis-à-vis the FRY, the EU failed to connect the question of acknowledging the FRY with the recognition of human and minority rights. Any further step towards cooperation and integration should therefore be linked to precise preconditions, which include the protection of human rights and steps towards a more far-reaching federalisation of the FRY.

A security pact with Russia and the CIS

Five years after the collapse of the USSR the development of the post-Soviet Central and Eastern European space is characterised by far-reaching contradictions, which have been intensified by Russian hegemonic demands. In view of Moscow's threats to link the eastern enlargement of NATO with the reintegration of the Commonwealth of Independent States (CIS), new escalations are in the offing. Three potential conflict regions could directly touch western interests: Ukraine, whose status as a state is still weak; the Caspian Sea and its rich energy reserves as well as the Russian minorities in Russia's CIS neighbour states.

At present democracy is not safe in any of the CIS members; more than anything, it is a stable institutional framework which is missing. Pauperisation and disillusionment of large parts of the population have seriously undermined democratic and economic reforms. A return to authoritarian rule with nationalist-xenophobic tendencies cannot be excluded. The economy does not only suffer from the effects of transformation-related recession: unstable banks, weak capital markets and a general uncertainty as far as the law is concerned make investment an uncalculable risk. In terms of foreign policy, due to a lack of political, economic and military resources Russia does not seem to be capable of bridging the gap between superpower pretensions and real resources in the medium term. Russia as it presents itself today, and the CIS directed by it will, in the long run, not be able to become either part or associated partner of the EU. European policy towards Eastern Europe must therefore develop a separate strategic framework of partnership and cooperation for this space.

The present agreements between the EU and the leading CIS members, as well as the "Action Plan for Russia", are not enough. Preferential treatment, which is included in the clause on a free-trade agreement, must be specifically extended for Russia and the "European" CIS members Belarus and Ukraine. Basically, the principle of equal treatment must be valid for Ukraine and Belarus. It is of major importance to develop the network of a trilateral security partnership with all three states – based on NATO and the OSCE and also involving the USA. Since, in the long term, the CIS will hardly survive as an integration community, it should not be upgraded by institutional contacts. Instead, the political stabilisation and national independence of individual CIS members ought to be specifically promoted. Russian efforts to enforce an old-style reintegration by means of military and security policy must be opposed by a western interest in a "new" superior integration community.

Future cooperation must be based on a redefinition of common security interests, which go beyond merely military threat perceptions. These interests should be fixed in a binding framework agreement between the USA, the EU and the three European CIS members. The development of such a "Strategic Security Pact" will play a key role in the relations between NATO and Russia. It would have to be complemented by parallel security treaties with Belarus and Ukraine. If this approach could be realised, it would also be possible to transform the contact group into a security council for Europe within the framework of the OSCE.

Despite possible setbacks, the West must cling to the aim of democratisation of Russia and the western CIS republics. The EU, as the European partner, is the most important coordinator of programmes for democratic support. Beyond the "Action Plan for Russia", and the one planned for Ukraine, the European Union should fix contacts with Russia, Belarus and Ukraine on several specialised and ministerial levels within the framework of a "structured dialogue". Ultimately, the future of the successor states of the USSR cannot be guaranteed by external financial aid. However, international financial transfer can, to a certain degree, balance deficits and fluctuations in the structural policy. The IMF must deliberately develop its role within this framework. The World Bank, the European Bank for Reconstruction and Development and the TACIS programme of the EU should support structural reforms more strongly than at present. The focus of the EU partnership agreement ought to be placed on the elimination of the remaining obstacles to investment. A further opening of western markets is more decisive than all regulatory intervention. A free-trade agreement between the EU, Russia, Belarus and Ukraine is the most important long-term aim. Liberal trade policy remains the best means to support the efforts made by Russia, Ukraine and Belarus as well, to be accepted into the World Trade Organisation (WTO).

Overcoming new borders

The Union needs calculable and reliable partners at its future borders. In addition to its strategies for enlargement, peace and partnership pursued within the framework of its policy towards Eastern Europe on the three different Eastern European spaces, European *Ostpolitik* must early on work out a concept for overall European neighbourhood, in order to balance the differences in stability and prosperity that exist along the future borders in the east and southeast of the EU. With this aim in view, forms of transnational cooperation must be supported now.

Intensified cooperation and networking activities in the newly developing Eastern European regions cannot be limited to regional initiatives. In an enlarged EU, security and stability will be based on the ability of the future EU member states to develop a policy of good-neighbourly relations at their eastern and southeastern borders. Western European states in the EU have grown together mainly at their borders. Cross-border cooperation between regions and communities has become an integral part of European unification. The model of Euro-regions should be extended to the neighbouring zones of the future EU.

Road, rail, energy and communication networks planned within the framework of Transeuropean Networks are of major importance for an overall European network. They form a crucial basis for the development of economic prosperity across Europe. The CIS and the Balkans should be included in planning the network.

Ultimately, Europe cannot merely be networked in the technical sense, it needs closer political interdependence. European policy towards Eastern Europe should cultivate forms of cooperation based on the model of the "Weimar Triangle" between France, Germany and Poland.

This new European *Ostpolitik* shows the way into an all-European future: the strategy for enlargement opens the perspective of an efficient EU from Sicily to the North Cape, and from the Atlantic to the river Bug. The Balkan strategy obliges the EU to uphold peace and economic modernisation in the southeast of Europe. The concept for partnership with Russia and the CIS guarantees closer ties of the post-Soviet CEE space to Europe. The concept for overall European neighbourhood defuses tensions between the spaces structured in this way. The European Union is the economic and political centre of the Continent – with this *Ostpolitik* it can implement a coherent concept for Europe as a whole. The risks call for, the chances warrant European action.

Preface

After the radical historic changes of 1989, Europe has experienced a time of transformation and uncertainties. In Eastern Europe a threefold transformation process started: from dictatorship to democracy, from planned economy to market economy and from a structure of joint policies to national independence. The collapse of the old order has not only produced a vacuum of political structures; guiding principles and societal orientation are also lacking. Most of the Eastern European governments try to adopt western institutions of democracy and market economy. Proposals for a "third way" are rejected. Many are not aware that the implicit confidence placed in them is an exceptional asset, which can be exhausted if expectations are not fulfilled and hopes are disappointed.

Compared with the reconstruction in Western Europe, the western community reacted too passively to the radical changes in Eastern Europe. To date, an overall strategic concept which sets political priorities and develops coordinated aid programmes is still missing. Instead, short-sighted considerations of vested interests impede the historically unique project of all-European unification. The speed and the course of the transformation processes divide the east of Europe into three political and economic spaces. Whereas the transformation of system is quickly progressing in the ten Central and Eastern European states associated with the EU, the countries of the Balkans as well as Russia and the CIS are falling behind.

The study outlines the concept for a new *Ostpolitik* which shows the way into an all-European future. The first chapter delineates the most important lines of development and the focal structural problems in the three Eastern European spaces. The second chapter describes which risks would result if the transformation of system in Eastern Europe failed. The third chapter is concentrated on the aims of a new *Ostpolitik* and on a critical stock-taking of past and present western aid for Eastern Europe. The concept of a new *Ostpolitik* for all-European development is presented in the fourth chapter. Three specific strategies are designed for the respective Eastern European spaces: a strategy for enlargement for Central and Eastern Europe, a strategy for peace for the Balkans and a strategy for cooperation and partnership for Russia and the CIS. Finally a concept for transnational, all-European neighbourhood aimed at creating a network between the different spaces is described.

The concept was worked out by the Research Group on European Affairs at the Center for Applied Policy Research of the University of Munich. It extrapolates the strategic recommendations which were formulated in 1992 in the publication "Eastern Europe: Challenges – Problems – Strategies" for the years to come. Both studies are results of the research project "Strategies for Europe"; within its framework the Research Group on European Affairs and the Bertelsmann Science Foundation jointly develop concepts which are aimed at supporting transformation towards market economy and democracy in Eastern Europe. The focus of the common project work is placed on integrating the Central and Eastern European states into the EU, defusing minority conflicts in Central and Eastern Europe and in the Balkans and establishing the trilateral security dialogue between America, Europe and Russia. The concept takes up the results of numerous conferences and discussions, in which – within the framework of the research project "Strategies for Europe" – high-ranking representatives from politics and academia regularly take part.

Professor Dr. Dr. h.c. Werner Weidenfeld
Member of the Board of the Bertelsmann Foundation
Director of the Center for Applied Policy Research (C.A.P.)
at the Ludwig-Maximilians-University of Munich

I. Situation

Diverging transformation processes divide the east of Europe into three political and economic spaces. Whereas in the ten Central and Eastern European states associated with the EU transformation is making quick progress, the countries of the Balkans as well as Russia and the CIS are falling behind in their development.

1. Central and Eastern Europe

The biggest progress in the transformation process has been made in the ten Central and European states (CEE) associated with the European Union.[1] In contrast to Russia, the CIS and the Balkan countries, these states have continuously gained in stability since 1989 and are now approximating the EU in economic, political and legal terms. Taking the economic and political consolidation of the transformation process into account, it can well be said that the reforms towards market economy and democracy will be consistently continued despite increasing social tensions. In all Central and Eastern European states the political élites keep up the reform course taken. All reform measures are directed to-

---

1 Bulgaria, the Czech Republic, Estonia, Hungary, Latvia, Lithuania, Poland, Romania, the Slovak Republic, and Slovenia.

wards a further approximation to Western European standards; their aim is the final "return to Europe" by integrating into the political and economic structures of Western Europe. The essential steps in this context are the Association Agreements with the EU, the NATO "Partnership for Peace" programme (PfP) and the Association Agreements with the WEU. It is mainly the perspective of full EU membership, included in the Association Agreements, which contributes to keeping the continuity of the restructuring and modernisation processes dynamic. However, the constant reform successes of the associated states are increasingly contrasted by the EU's own lack of reform capacity.

All Central and Eastern European states have overcome the low of the recession caused by transformation, and thanks to the positive development of their macroeconomic data, they have gained in economic stability since 1994. Nevertheless, because of different conditions at the start, the speed and extent of the transformation processes still differ. There is no doubt that the Czech Republic, Hungary, Poland, the Slovak Republic, Slovenia and Estonia belong into the group of economically successful states. The economic framework data of the Czech Republic are in parts already better than those of some of the EU member states so that in the near future the country might fulfil the convergence criteria for participation in European economic and monetary union. By virtue of its successful reform policy, the Czech Republic was the first Central and Eastern European country to be accepted into the OECD in November 1995. As regards the standard of living, according to the most recent OECD economic survey the conditions for a steady and speedy approximation to the other OECD countries are fulfilled in this country.[2]

Since 1989 Central and Eastern Europe has become a first-rate growth area. In comparison to the year before, economic growth further increased in 1995 in almost all states of this region (with the exception of Latvia, Slovenia and Hungary). The average growth of the real gross national product (GNP) was 5.2 percent (1994: 4 percent).[3] With an aver-

---

2 Cf. OECD: OECD Economic Surveys: The Czech Republic 1996, Paris 1996.
3 The following data have been taken from: European Commission: European Economy. Economic situation and economic reform in Central and Eastern Europe. Supplement C. Economic Reform Monitor No. 1 – May 1996, Luxembourg 1996. Cf. also World Bank: World Development Report, Washington 1996.

age GNP growth of 7 percent, Poland, Romania and the Slovak Republic were in the lead among the reform states. According to the first forecasts, the region can again count on an average growth of almost 5 percent for 1996 and 1997. Progress is made in checking inflation rates although, to date, in none of the reform states has a stable price development been reached. In 1995 the Czech and the Slovak Republic could for the first time reach single-digit inflation rates, which, however, in comparison with the EU average are still too high. In 1995 the latecomers Bulgaria and Romania succeeded in reducing their inflation rates to 62 and 33 percent respectively. As privatisation has not yet been finished, the danger of growing unemployment rates is looming in all Central and Eastern European states (at present they vary between 3 percent in the Czech Republic and 15 percent in Poland). The share of the private sector in GNP is between 50 to 80 percent in Poland, Estonia, the Czech Republic and Hungary. By contrast, in Bulgaria and Romania privatisation is still developing slowly with a share of 30 to 40 percent.

Exports towards Western Europe, which have strongly increased, as well as national and international direct investment are of major importance for the growth in Central and Eastern Europe. Approximately 50 percent of the exports of the ten associated countries have meanwhile been going into the EU. Germany has become the most important trading partner and the most strongly committed foreign investor in the region. With an accumulated net foreign capital inflow of approximately US$ 13.1 bn from 1990 to mid-1995, Hungary, Poland and the Czech Republic are the top receivers of direct investment. With US$ 7.4 bn Hungary was able to attract more than half of this foreign direct investment.[4] Since 1995 economic growth in Central and Eastern Europe has increasingly been supported by domestic demand.

In Central and Eastern Europe infrastructure is better developed and the economic structure is already more differentiated than in other Eastern European regions – these are additional factors favouring the boom in Central and Eastern Europe. The share of the service sector and of tourism in GNP (reaching up to 60 percent) has clearly increased in all

---

4 As for the data on foreign direct investment cf. UN-ECE: Economic Bulletin for Europe Vol. 47, New York 1995, p. 104.

CEE states – in particular in the Baltic states. By contrast the share of agriculture has visibly decreased. The agricultural sector continues to play an important role only in Poland, where approximately 25 percent of the population are still working in agriculture, which is characterised by smallholdings. New industries (electronics, chemical industry) producing high-quality exports are gaining increasingly more importance in the progressive reform states.

Meanwhile the CEE states' trade with the former Soviet partners in the Council for Mutual Economic Assistance (Comecon) has constantly been decreasing. Despite several tendencies towards recovery in the exchange with Russia, trade with western partners more and more determines the course of the future EU accession states. The previously existing, almost complete dependence in the energy sector is also decreasing as for political reasons the more successful CEE states diversify their supply sources.[5] At the same time Central and Eastern Europe are gaining increasing importance as industrial location for Western European enterprises. A well-trained workforce, the geographic proximity to the EU and the relatively low real wage level in labour-intensive industrial branches encourage investors.

In the Baltic states, Bulgaria and Romania these favourable location factors are still impaired by several obstacles (slow public administrations, legal uncertainty, shortcomings in the infrastructure, deficits in the banking and loan sector). Thus, to date, the financing needed for modernisation in these countries could only insufficiently be covered by foreign investment (accumulated until mid-1995 approximately US$ 2.1 bn). In Slovakia the unstable political situation and the obscure privatisation policy also result in relatively low foreign direct investment. In 1995 Slovakia was the only CEE state to record a stagnation in foreign capital inflow.[6]

In contrast to the states of the former Soviet Union or the Balkans, the economic stabilisation in Central and Eastern Europe offers favourable preconditions for further democratic consolidation. The development of democratic political systems, characterised by party pluralism, the division of power, free and secret elections and the respect for general prin-

---

5 Cf. Clement, Hermann: Integrations- und Desintegrationstendenzen in Osteuropa und der GUS, Working Paper No.1 186, Osteuropa-Institut, Munich, December 1995.
6 Cf. Handelsblatt of 11 March 1996.

ciples of law, has made considerable progress. In the more progressive CEE states intermediary authorities, such as parties, trade unions and independent media, have also developed in a positive way.[7] However, the confrontation course of Slovak domestic policy raises doubts about the democratic development of the country. In 1995 the EU lodged two diplomatic protests expressing its worries about the internal situation in Slovakia and pointing out that the country's political course might delay its being integrated into the EU.

In none of the Central and Eastern European states is the formation of governments by post-communist forces – as in Poland and Hungary – linked to a revival of communist ideologies. None of the leading parties questions the reform course directed towards market economy and democracy or the ties with Western Europe. The election of post-communist candidates, who promise more social security, is rather to be seen as the population's reaction to the increasing societal and psychological-social costs of the transformation (declining income, unemployment).

The growing social tensions in all Central and Eastern European states are the greatest danger to democratisation. The transformation is accompanied by increasing social uncertainty and inequality. Income and the standard of living have slumped: today a quarter of the people in Central and Eastern Europe live below the poverty line. The unemployed, pensioners and large families with only one earner are most heavily affected. In Bulgaria 70 percent of the population live either on the threshold of, or below, the poverty line.[8] With the constantly widening earnings gap the crime rate also spreads. In almost all CEE states an increasing dissatisfaction with the new political institutions has become manifest. The disappointment results in people becoming frustrated with politics and in low turnouts at the elections. Many voters do not expect politics to improve their situation.[9]

All over Eastern Europe the end of communism has led to a renaissance of ethnic-nationally determined interests. The historical experi-

---

7 Cf. Weidenfeld, Werner (ed.): Central and Eastern Europe on the Way into the European Union, Gütersloh 1994ff.
8 Cf. Božidar, Šabev: 7 miliona živejat bedno, in: Kontinent of 15 July 1996, p. 7.
9 Cf. Rose, Richard: Mobilizing demobilized voters in post-communist societies, in: Party Politics No. 4, 1995, pp. 549–563.

ence of the Central and Eastern European states, which for centuries had been dominated by imperial powers (Russia, Prussia, Austria) and, since 1945, had been subject to Soviet rule, was characterised by the loss of their national independence. Whereas the collapse of the multinational state of Yugoslavia resulted in war and bloodshed, the detachment of the three Baltic states from the former Soviet Union (1991) and the separation of the former CSSR into the Czech and the Slovak Republics (1993) came about peacefully. Slovenia declared its independence in 1991. Defusing the tensions between national sovereignty and European integration will become difficult for these states, in which a new national awareness has only recently developed. EU membership requires that they accept the complete acquis communautaire of the Union with all its set norms and common aims. Participation in the European single market would above all demand that the Central and Eastern European states develop an enormous set of regulations.

The existence of ethnically heterogeneous states is another characteristic of Central and Eastern Europe.[10] With the exceptions of Hungary, Poland and the Czech Republic, states made up of different nationalities, each with shares of minorities of more than 10 percent, predominate this region. The group of ethnic Russians makes up 33.8 percent of the overall population in Latvia, 30.3 percent in Estonia and 9.4 percent in Lithuania. In recent years some Central and Eastern European states have found more or less promising approaches in their national legislation in order to settle minority conflicts. However, there are still considerable problems as regards the Hungarian minorities in Slovakia (11 percent) and Romania (8 percent). The mutual ratification of the basic treaty is an important breakthrough for Slovak-Hungarian relations. The amendment to the Slovak State Language Act in November 1995, however, has again put a strain on relations between the two states as regulations for the protection of the minority languages were annulled. The road for a basic treaty between Hungary and Romania was cleared only after both sides added that they guarantee collective minority rights and territorial autonomy on ethnic grounds. The restitution of Hungarian church property and the reopening of the Hungarian university in Cluj still remain disputed.

---

10 Cf. Brunner, Georg: Nationality Problems and Minority Conflicts in Eastern Europe, Gütersloh 1996.

In terms of foreign policy the orientation of the Central and Eastern European states has changed fundamentally since the events of 1989. The objective of the "return to Europe" is the re-establishment of historical and cultural ties and the political, economic and military integration into Western institutions. The major foreign policy aim of the CEE states is membership of the EU and NATO. Regional cooperation patterns – such as the Central European Free-Trade Area (CEFTA), founded in 1993, or the Baltic Free-Trade Area (1994)[11] – are not considered as real alternatives to EU integration. On the contrary, the newly created regional structures encounter obstacles. In its dynamic, CEFTA in particular has not come up to the initial expectations. Go-it-alone approaches and competitive thinking instead of political cooperation and solidarity determine the activities of the individual members. In addition, intraregional trade could hardly be stimulated due to the mainly complementary economic structures. To date intraregional trade has made up only a small share (5–10 percent) of the aggregate trade volume of the CEFTA states. Due to parallel economic structures trade among the Baltic states is also heavily underdeveloped.[12]

The ten CEE states have been given a firm option for joining the European Union by the Association Agreements[13] provided they can fulfil the criteria for accession which were determined at the Copenhagen summit in 1993. Since, however, neither the schedule nor the organisation of future enlargement rounds have been fixed until now, the perspective of the Central and Eastern European countries' accession remains unclear. All ten associated states have already applied for accession, with Slovenia bringing up the rear in June 1996. Accession will not be possible before the structural reform of the EU; it cannot be envisaged before the year 2000. According to the decision of the Madrid summit of December 1995, the first negotiations for accession are to be entered into six months after the end of the Intergovernmental Conference on the revision of the Maastricht Treaty (IGC), i.e. presumably at the end of

---

11 Poland, Hungary, the Czech and the Slovak Republics as well as Slovenia (since January 1996) are among the members of CEFTA.
12 Cf. Meier, Christian: Wirtschaftsbeziehungen zwischen den Staaten Osteuropas: Regionale Kooperation auf dem Prüfstand, in: Berichte BIOst No. 36, 1995.
13 Cf. also table 1 in the annex: state of the Association Agreements of the EU with the Central and Eastern European states.

1997/beginning of 1998. As for the eastern enlargement of NATO, on the other hand, concrete steps will certainly be taken sooner. Chances are good for Poland, Hungary and the Czech Republic to be accepted into NATO before the year 2000.

Accession to the EU and NATO is highly advocated by the populations in almost all CEE states (90 percent of the population approve of EU integration; 82 percent of NATO integration), which shows the popularity of integration into western structures governments are aiming at.[14] Romania (97 percent) and Poland (93 percent) view EU integration most favourably; in Estonia and Slovenia respectively approximately 76 percent agree to it. However, despite the positive basic attitude, there is still a lack of concrete notions about the EU, its policies and institutions as well as costs and benefits of EU accession in all states. In addition, the reputation of the EU has noticeably worsened since 1995, in particular in Lithuania, Bulgaria, the Czech Republic and Slovakia. Many people do not expect that relations with the EU will improve their own living conditions, instead they believe that the necessary adjustment will cause additional hardships. NATO membership is most strictly rejected by the Bulgarian population: only 52 percent advocate NATO accession whereas 48 percent come out against it. Government circles also differ considerably in their opinion about the speed and the form of a potential NATO membership: whereas the president in office at the moment and the opposition speak out in favour of unconditional and speedy integration into NATO, the ruling socialists have not yet declared a clear position.

2. The Balkans

For many Western Europeans the Balkan region, unlike Central and Eastern Europe, still means backwardness, war and irreconcilable ethnic conflicts. At a closer look, however, big cultural, social, economic and

---

14 As for the following survey results cf. European Commission: Eurobarometer survey Central and Eastern Europe, Brussels March 1996.

political differences between the Southeast European countries become visible so that one can hardly speak of "the" Balkans. Whenever the Balkans or the Balkan countries are mentioned here, we are primarily dealing with Albania, Bosnia-Herzegovina, the Federal Republic of Yugoslavia (Serbia and Montenegro; subsequently FRY), Croatia and the former Yugoslav Federal Republic of Macedonia (subsequently Macedonia). Slovenia, Bulgaria and Romania, which are usually counted among the Balkans, signed Association Agreements with the EU and thus have a firm prospect of EU membership. Therefore these countries, as well as Greece and Turkey with their different problems, will only be touched upon in passing in this context.

The Balkan region historically developed in an area of tensions between Christian-Occidental, Orthodox-Byzantine and Islamic hegemonic powers and cultures. Due to this development it is characterised by numerous cultural, religious and linguistic traditions and influences. As these characteristics, which form identity and group solidarity, are not clear-cut in most population groups, it is possible to question almost all attempts at nation-building simply by pointing out other uniting traits. Croats, Bosniaks and Serbs differ by religion but not by language; Slovenes and Croats have the same (Catholic) denomination but no common language, as is the case with Macedonians and Serbs. Montenegrans and Serbs, by contrast, only trace their different identities back to a diverging history. In addition, the individual ethnic groups do not live in compact territories but in scattered settlement areas. In the Balkans the establishment of modern nation states has therefore long been delayed; it is still a tedious process abounding in conflicts.

Nation-building is a challenge to the existing borders. Since nationalist blueprints were spread in the 19th century, ethnic differences have repeatedly escalated into violent conflicts. However, potential ethnic conflicts in the Balkans are not a predetermined cultural-anthropological condition. It is rather the political élites who, greedy for power, stress the ethnic dimension, thus intensifying existing conflicts of interests in order to mobilise support. Violent outbursts, seemingly archaic, usually hide rational political calculations. By instrumentalising ethnic differences, i. e. by consciously charging politics with ethnic contents, the differences in the Balkans are becoming extremely virulent.

With the end of the communist rule the "Yugoslav experiment", i. e. the attempt at integrating different ethnic identities into a federalist system, failed.[15] The nation-state projects of the new political élites were accompanied by discrimination and oppression of ethnic minorities, and, in the worst case, by "ethnic cleansing". In the collapsing Yugoslavia a destructive reciprocity evolved between the republics' policy of autonomy, on the one hand, and the threat perceptions of ethnic groups on the other hand. The war in Bosnia-Herzegovina, which eradicated the fundament of multi-ethnic coexistence, was the worst result produced by this dynamism. The peace order determined in the Dayton accords was made possible only by massive deployment of military forces by the West; it has until today suffered from the local élites' unwillingness to cooperate. The presence of the international "Stabilisation Force" (SFOR) troops is the only guarantee for a peaceful coexistence of the different population groups. The civil agreements of the Dayton accords and the Bosniak-Croat federation have only been realised in their initial stages.

Apart from the problems in Bosnia-Herzegovina there are further unsolved minority problems and ethnic conflicts: the question of the Serb minority in East Slavonia; the status of the Albanian population groups in Kosovo and Macedonia; the rights of the Greek minority in Albania; the Hungarian minority in Vojvodina and the Muslim minority in the Sandzak.

This only accounts for those ethnic groups which have politically organised themselves and articulated their interests. However, due to the historically scattered settlement structures the region is even more heterogeneous.

All Balkan countries follow the transformation course towards market economy, with considerable differences in their respective starting situation. While the successor states of the former Yugoslavia can refer to a tradition of free-enterprise reforms and opening towards foreign economies, Albania must overcome a Stalinist economic pattern which isolated the state from the outside to a high degree. At the beginning of the 1990s the whole region started to suffer from a deep recession with de-

---

15 Cf. Sundhausen, Holm: Experiment Jugoslawien. Von der Staatsgründung bis zum Zerfall, Mannheim 1993.

creasing production, increasing unemployment, growing inflation and deteriorating trade balances. The causes must be seen in the destructions of the war and the ensuing collapse of production, in trade embargoes (on the FRY and Macedonia), but also in the restrictive stabilisation policy which was introduced by Albania, Croatia and Macedonia in context with their free-enterprise reforms.

Albania, Croatia and Macedonia, like the more advanced states of Central and Eastern Europe, have been able to improve their macroeconomic situation within recent years. They have registered considerable progress mainly in the privatisation of small businesses. While the privatisation of large state-owned enterprises is making only slow progress, the private sector is quickly expanding. The share of the private sector in the gross national product is estimated at 45 percent for Croatia, 35 percent for Macedonia, and at even approximately 50 percent for Albania (reference year 1994).[16] Although part of the new entrepreneurs hardly correspond with western patterns, and many of their business ideas will fail, a new economic élite and a societal group interested in structures operating under the rule of law might emerge from among them. At present, however, foreign investors consider the Balkan region as politically unstable and a peripheral market. They participate in privatisation only to a small extent; foreign direct investment has also, until now, scantily flown into the region. Between 1992 and June 1995, Albania, Croatia and Macedonia could attract foreign investment amounting to US$ 154 m, US$ 127 m and US$ 5 m respectively, whereas in Bulgaria and Poland, for example, approximately US$ 300 m and US$ 1.7 bn respectively were invested.[17]

A western-style modernisation in the Balkan region is impeded by significant economic structural deficits. The differences in economic development run along a rough line from the northwest (Slovenia) to the southeast (Kosovo, Albania, Macedonia). In comparison to the more successful Central and Eastern European states, the Balkan countries have for a long time played a marginal role within the European eco-

---

16 Cf. Frankfurter Allgemeine Zeitung Informationsdienste (ed.): Osteuropa-Perspektiven – Jahrbuch 1995/96, Frankfurt 1995; cf. also österreichisches Institut für Wirtschaftsforschung (ed.): The Economies of Central and Eastern Europe, Recent Trends and Prospects for 1996, Vienna 1996.
17 Cf. UN-ECE: Economic Bulletin for Europe Vol. 47, 1995, p. 104.

nomic division of labour. Even though Albania remains the only classically agricultural country, the share of agriculture in the gross national product in the other countries is also considerably above EU average. Productivity and the standard of technology in industrial enterprises are low, outmoded heavy industries with a high consumption of raw material prevail.[18] There is a lack of qualified workers and the educational systems are insufficiently developed. Tourism doubtlessly offers a high potential for development to the Mediterranean countries Croatia, Albania and Montenegro – however, one-sided dependence on tourism and agriculture harbours many problems. At present the infrastructural preconditions to develop modern industries do not yet exist. Although Croatia and Serbia are in a slightly more favourable situation than the other Balkan countries, structural problems prevent all Balkan states from quickly approximating to EU level.

In the Balkans, as in all transformation states of Eastern Europe, an extensive "shadow economy" exists beside the state and private economy. In Macedonia, for example, it accounts for approximately 40 percent of GDP.[19] Employment in this sector certainly allows large population groups to earn their living, but also obstructs the functioning of labour markets, efficiency improvements in the official economy and macroeconomic stabilisation policies. The living standard of the population decreases while earnings gaps and poverty increase. In Croatia alone real income halved between 1989 and 1994.[20]

Compared to the Central and Eastern European states, the Balkan countries are characterised by high political instability. At present their political systems resemble western parliamentary democracies only on the surface, at best. The post-communist structures have not yet become legitimate institutions firmly anchored in everyday practice. The recent Albanian riots caused by the collapse of several pyramid investment schemes have shown that many Albanian citizens hold the government directly responsible for the bankruptcy of business firms, thus sustaining the close link between state and economy common in the communist

---

18 Cf. Neue Zürcher Zeitung of 22 April 1996; Oschlies, Wolf: Ex-Jugoslawien '95. Politisch-ökonomische Portraits der sechs Nachfolgestaaten, in: Berichte des BIOst No. 54, 1995.
19 Cf. Handelsblatt of 14 February 1996.
20 Oschlies, Wolf, ibd., p. 18.

system. Few people trust in politicians and parliaments. They have little reason to do so as incumbents are inclined to abuse their constitutional powers to change the rules of political competition. This was bluntly demonstrated by the failed attempt of the Serbian socialists to falsify local election results. Authoritarian-charismatic personalities, such as the Croat and Serb leaders Tudjman and Milosevic, have hitherto dominated political life. It is uncertain whether the current opposition will be able to replace them by leaders who embody a democratic political style. In the parties as well as within government and administration many political decision-making processes are based on paternalistic and clientelist structures. Public administration works inefficiently and is handicapped by corruption and nepotism.

In the Balkans the development of democratic institutions working under the rule of law has reached different stages. However, unlike in Central and Eastern Europe, such institutions have not yet been consolidated or integrated into the political culture in any of the states. Weeks of demonstrations in Belgrade and other Serb cities showed the emergence of a citizens' movement that questioned the legitimacy of the Milosevic régime. The movement succeeded in attaining recognition of the local election results of November 1996, which, in the major cities of the country, were won by the opposition coalition Zajedno.[21] However, civil society – the network of public debate, intermediary institutions and autonomous political actors – is still weak in the region. Civic actors and movements can only bring about a gradual democratisation, and still do not have sufficient influence to bind political power to the constitution. This weakness is symptomatic for the fragile Balkan states which are not able to create the preconditions for a strong civil society by rigorous economic reforms and administrative rationalisation.

Croatia, Macedonia, Bosnia-Herzegovina and Albania strive for concluding EU Association Agreements, joining the European Union and being integrated into NATO. Macedonia and Albania have already signed cooperation agreements with the EU and take part in the "Partnership for Peace" programme of NATO. Since 1995 Albania has been a member of the Council of Europe; Macedonia, having guest status, applied for mem-

---

21 Cf. Frankfurter Allgemeine Zeitung of 5 February 1997.

bership. The Council of Europe accepted Croatia under the condition that it observes the Dayton accords. All four Balkan countries are members of the OSCE. In addition Albania is a member of the Islamic League and, like Bosnia-Herzegovina, maintains good relations with some Islamic countries. The FRY presently endeavours to put an end to its international isolation. It wants to succeed the former Yugoslavia in the OSCE, the World Bank and the International Monetary Fund (IMF). Serbia has special historical ties with Russia, which, after a long period of Yugoslav-Soviet differences, were revived during the war in Bosnia.

3. Russia and the CIS

Compared to the Central and Eastern European states, the political and economic transformation in Russia and the other states of the CIS is considerably lagging behind. In almost all fields of transformation, from macroeconomic stabilisation to the consolidation of democratic institutions, the former superpower Russia has fallen far behind the former Central and Eastern European "brother countries". Whereas the CEE states have continued to register economic growth rates since 1993/94, Russia and the other CIS members will need much more time to pass through the economic trough. Before the hoped-for boom another period of drawn-out political and economic crisis is imminent in Russia and most of the CIS member states. If this development continues, the economic space of the CIS is threatened to disintegrate from the advanced integration structures of the west.

The diverging development is mainly due to different historical and structural starting conditions. The legacy of the Soviet, and also of the pre-communist, past is much bigger in Russia and the other states of the former USSR than in Central and Eastern Europe. None of the CIS members could draw from former experiences with reforms and democracy, or from a politico-economic culture, which have been important reasons for the transformation successes in the CEE states since 1989. Moreover, the distance between the consistently reformist states in Central and

Eastern Europe ("shock therapy") and the "slow reformers" in the CIS space is growing.[22] Transformation progress is also retarded by the absence of an external anchor to reform and integration, such as the EU with its integration strategy and the prospect of membership for the CEE states. Furthermore the Commonwealth of Independent States (CIS) does not offer a clear and desirable integration perspective to the new states of the post-Soviet space.

The most important deficit the reform course is suffering from, however, is the lack of consensus in the populations about what constitutes national identity. This affects internal as well as external relations. In Russia, in particular, the basic transformation of the nation-state framework has not yet been achieved. There is neither a consensus on Russia's internal identity nor on who are to be Russia's partners in its new foreign policy. Whereas the states of Central and Eastern Europe have regained their national identity, the majority of Russians still consider the collapse of the Soviet Empire a loss and a national disaster. The simultaneous loss of imperial supremacy, the status of international superpower and the security policy glacis in East Central Europe; the separation of the Slav "sister republics" Belarus and Ukraine; as well as the diaspora of more than 20 million Russians living beyond the new borders still have lasting traumatic effects in Russia.

National identity is also often lacking in the new CIS members. As nation states almost all republics are latecomers and their nation-building process is as yet far from completed. In the current transition period they remain disoriented as regards their role in the post-Soviet world. In view of the difficult transformation years disillusionment and disappointment have increased in all Eastern European reform states, but individual CIS member states remain caught in a "vicious circle of nostalgia" to a greater extent than others.[23] Open revisionist tendencies exist in Belarus,

---

22 Cf. World Bank: From Plan to Market, World Development Report 1996, Washington 1996, pp. 22ff. This opinion is also held by Åslund, Anders: Reform vs. "Rent-Seeking" in Russia's Economic Transformation, in: Transition 26 January 1996.
23 According to a survey at the beginning of 1996, 72 percent of the Russians interviewed wished to return to the Soviet economic system; in the Czech Republic, by contrast, meanwhile 63 percent have said they were in favour of the new system. Cf. Havlik, Peter: Uncertain Recovery Prospects in Russia, in: Vienna Institute for Comparative Economic Studies (ed.): The Vienna Institute Monthly Report No. 4, 1996, Vienna 1996.

but also in Russia. The future of the post-Soviet region considerably depends on what will be more important for Russia and its CIS neighbours: a new way of thinking or old myths from the past.

In terms of economic policy the development in the CIS has taken a contradictory course. Russia has managed to catch up with the successful transformation states in only some areas: thus the share of the quickly growing non-state sector in the Russian GDP is moving closer to the success rates in Central and Eastern Europe (estimates range between 30 and 65 percent). The radical reorientation in foreign trade is another important parallel: today Russia carries out more than 50 percent of its trade with the European Union whereas trade within the CIS is continuously decreasing (1995: 17 percent). In contrast to Central and Eastern Europe, progress in this and other areas (debt conversion, falling budget deficit) is not supported by increasing domestic demand and growing gross investment in Russia and in the other CIS members. Now as before, a reliable free-enterprise framework for further transformation progress is still missing in all CIS members.

Contrary to forecasts by leading western institutions, the economies of Russia and most CIS members have, so far, not shown any positive change. In contrast to Central and Eastern Europe, the GDP of Russia and its most important neighbour states has further decreased in the sixth year after the political change.[24] Even if in 1997 small growth were achieved for the first time, this would not (yet) be a sufficient impulse for a trend reversal. The experience of the Central and Eastern European associated states shows that even continuous growth rates of 5 percent are not enough speedily to bridge the gap to the western industrial states.

In most of the other successor states of the Soviet Union economic growth has also been decreasing further. With the exception of some positive tendencies in Armenia (which was the first CIS member to register positive growth rates since 1994), Moldavia and Uzbekistan, there has not, as yet, been any real perspective for the other CIS states to catch up on their economic development in years to come. In 1996 the Interna-

---

24 Podkaminer, Leon et al.: Continuing Improvements in Central and Eastern Europe – Russia and Ukraine Have not yet Turned the Corner, in: Vienna Institute for Comparative Economic Studies (ed.); Research Report No. 225, February 1996.

tional Monetary Fund and the European Bank for Reconstruction and Development (EBRD) forecast an average economic growth of 0.3 percent at best for the whole CIS space – in contrast to a growth of 3 to 6 percent for the CEE states. However, in most CIS republics economies continue to decline. Meanwhile, the developing gap between Central and Eastern Europe and the CIS members keeps growing.

Instead of the "Iron Curtain" of the post-war period a new political, economic and socio-cultural cleavage threatens to develop at the future eastern borders of the European Union. Even today the political instability in the post-Soviet space is far greater than in Central and Eastern Europe. Unlike the CEE states, several CIS republics have taken disquieting steps backwards as far as the formation of pluralist societies is concerned.[25] Unreformed authoritarian regimes have consolidated their power in the Central Asian republics; but in the future EU neighbour states Russia and Belarus considerable democratic deficits are also visible.

In all CIS countries the social crisis is much more far-reaching than in Central and Eastern Europe. Therefore free-enterprise reforms are rejected in the countries of the former Soviet Union to a greater extent than in the CEE states.[26] At the same time readiness for polarisation, internal conflict and the use of force increases. The war in Chechnya and the numerous smouldering conflicts in the remaining CIS space indicate that another dividing line has evolved which separates the regions of Central and Eastern Europe from the CIS (and the Balkans as well). Since 1991, due to internal conflicts and ethnic tensions, more than nine million people have been fleeing from their homes within the CIS.[27] This has been the biggest migration wave since the end of World War II. If the CIS space cannot be stabilised permanently, the gigantic flow of refugees will certainly swell further. This could also entail incalculable consequences for the West.

---

25 According to the analyses of the American human rights organisation Freedom House, compliance with political rights and civil liberties worsened in eight CIS republics between 1991 and 1995; it improved only in four CIS republics – Armenia, Georgia, Kirghizia and Moldavia. Cf. Freedom House: Nations in Transit, New York 1995.
26 Cf. Gati, Charles: The Mirage of Democracy, in: Transition 22 March 1996.
27 Cf. data of the UN Office of the High Commissioner for Refugees (UNHCR) at an international conference on refugees and expellees in the CIS, Frankfurter Allgemeine Zeitung of 31 May 1996.

The development of the CIS makes for an important difference in the regional perspective: neither the integration agreement signed by four CIS republics (Russia, Belarus, Kazakhstan, Kirghizia) nor the pompously celebrated union treaty between Moscow and Minsk can delude observers as to the fact that the CIS remains restricted in its capacity for action and integration.[28] In the foreseeable future the CIS will not become a supra-national integration community along the lines of the EU. This is due to a series of factors, which will continue to characterise the specific development in the post-Soviet space:
- Real integration is mainly blocked by Russia itself. Russia is even less willing than other member states to give up parts of its national sovereignty in favour of a policy of integration towards the "near abroad". In its CIS policy the "old thinking" from Soviet times prevails: Russia does not want to integrate itself into a superior structure; it rather wants to unite the other CIS members under its aegis. Instead of integrating into new systems, Moscow more and more visibly strives for an old-style reintegration. The increasing bilateralisation of relations within the CIS is a symptom of this tendency: Moscow systematically develops bilateral agreements in order to promote a community centred around Russia, but other successor states also increasingly pursue bilateral contacts. The horizontal intertwinement necessary for a functioning integration community increasingly lags behind this development.
- The development of economic union, which could offer the CIS republics a promising perspective, has also got stuck at the beginning. Except for slow progress made in the establishment of a customs union, economic disintegration continues.[29] This is not only due to the fact that Russia has rigorously cut back subsidies and adapted its raw material deliveries to world market prices. The centrifugal forces in trade and in mutual financial relations within the CIS are also responsible for this development. For all successor states of the Soviet Union have one thing in common: like Russia, the other CIS members also purposefully orientate their trade increasingly towards the West.

---

28 Zagorski, Andrei: Die neuen "Unionen" in der GUS: Ernsthaft und auf Dauer?, in: Aktuelle Analysen des BIOst No. 38, 1996.
29 Clement, Hermann: ibd., p. 41.

II. Risks

In all three Central and Eastern European regions (Central and Eastern Europe, the Balkans, Russia and the CIS) positive developments are still counterbalanced by considerable risks, which differ in terms of mode and measure. While the effects of transformation create uncertainties in the associated states of Central and Eastern Europe, in the CIS and former Yugoslavia stability and peace are in danger.

1. Central and Eastern Europe

Stagnating modernisation and social conflicts

Despite the macroeconomic recovery the transformation process has not been completed in any state of Central and Eastern Europe. Further reforms of competition policy, legal systems, the financial sector and social policy are required in order to guarantee a permanent success of the free-enterprise transformation and the aspired integration into the EU. If reforms stagnated, this would not only delay the EU accession of these states but also endanger the whole course of the economic and political transformation in Eastern Europe. A destabilisation of the transformation process could intensify social tensions all over the region, give fresh impetus to populist forces and revive old myths. As an immediate consequence of renewed uncertainty about the further course of the transformation process, international investors would withdraw from the region and economic modernisation would slow down.

The European internal market in particular is a high obstacle for the Central and Eastern European countries. In case of an immediate integration, the existing differences in the competition, legal and financial systems would distort the terms of competition and severely restrict the functioning of the internal market. Temporarily suspending the rules of the internal market in order to facilitate accession for the CEE countries would, however, mean to revoke the Single Market. Competition is not regulated efficiently enough, which is a great impediment. In almost all Central and Eastern European states some parts of the markets are still exempt from competition and thus inaccessible. In the Baltic states, for instance, infrastructure is still excluded from competition. In some states, such as Romania, there are still a few subsidised prices for basic foodstuffs. Furthermore exchange rates and import duties are kept low in individual CEE states as a protection against foreign competitors. The necessary approximation of Eastern European laws to the extensive legislation of the European internal market is another great challenge.

In all Central and Eastern European states the old banking system, which dated from the times of planned economy, has been transformed into a two-tier system consisting of central banks and commercial banks. To date, however, the funding of the new banks has been insufficient. Moreover, due to a high percentage of irrecoverable debts claimed against state-owned companies many banks are in dire straits. In many cases the state as owner of the big banks still controls a great share of the lending business. What is more important is that none of the CEE states possesses an efficient bank supervision. The severe bank crises in Latvia and Lithuania in 1995 and in Bulgaria in 1996 were a warning to the whole region. If the highly critical development of the banking and financial sector continues, this could – by adding to the budget costs and increasing foreign debts – lead to a dangerous destabilisation of the reform processes. The dramatic political and economic developments in Bulgaria at the beginning of 1997 serve as a good example.

The growing social uncertainty is another risk factor. The increasing pauperisation of different sections of the population is a hotbed for disappointment and frustration, which could considerably weaken the social consensus with a view to further reforms. Due to falling incomes for a large part of the population and continuously high structural unemployment (approximately 15 percent in Poland, Slovenia and Slovakia), potential social conflicts will further increase. Until now a working social network based on the principle of insurance, social services and welfare has been missing in all CEE states. In addition, the continuously high unemployment and the expansion of the shadow economy result in declining contributions to the pension funds, which means it is evident even today that pension funding will run into difficulties. Moreover, the state of health of the populations has massively deteriorated due to the insufficient funding of public health services – the average spending on health does not account for more than 5 percent of GDP in Central and Eastern Europe, in the OECD countries it amounts to 8 percent. In Romania approximately 15 percent of the population are not or only partially fit for work.

Unstable economic systems, growing unemployment, overtaxed social security systems and the deep earnings gap between east and west in the CEE states not least increase the risk of a further migration into the more affluent West. People become more willing to move since they hope to find better opportunities for work and making money in the EU. If the prosperity gap deepens further, this will have serious consequences in particular for the eastern border regions of the EU states Germany, Austria and Italy, which would be directly affected by waves of people trying to escape from poverty and unfavourable economic conditions.

Environmental problems

In terms of ecology the entire Eastern European region has until now been one of the most severely polluted regions in the world. Despite an enormous need for redevelopment, the economic transformation has predominated over ecological modernisation after 1989. At the all-European environmental conference "Environment for Europe" in Sofia (October 1995), the financial requirements for environmental redevelopment in the next two decades was put at DM 250 bn for the Central and Eastern European region, and at DM 1,750 bn for the whole former Eastern bloc. Western assistance has up to now been able to cover only a small share of the necessary investment. From 1990 to 1995 environmental investment of just approximately ECU 3.7 bn flowed into Eastern Europe, 80 percent of which went to the Central and Eastern European countries.[30] If the improvement of environmental protection is further neglected, the environmental damages and the redevelopment costs necessary in order to repair them will assume alarming proportions for the West. The exploitation of natural resources in Central and Eastern Europe has long since crossed local and national borders and harbours grave consequences for overall Europe and the world (land degradation, change of climate). Much environmental damage threatens to become irreversible. A large number of animal and plant species in Eastern Europe is already in danger of becoming extinct.[31]

The severe environmental pollution in Central and Eastern Europe must be attributed to the inefficient use of resources, the lack of technologies reducing emission and insufficient institutional and legislative framework conditions. People's environmental awareness has until now been poor. Behaviour showing environmental awareness is not promoted by any form of incentive or information. In none of the Central and Eastern European countries has an influential environmental lobby been able to establish itself. Given the transnational impact of environmental pollution, better environmental protection in the region as well as cooperation in terms of environmental policy with the CEE states are particularly interesting for the EU.[32]

Core areas with a high concentration of pollutants are to be found in the north of the Czech Republic, in Slovakia and in the southwest of Poland. Due to the predominant use of coal for power production (approximately 80 percent) and the secondary charges of heavy industry, air pollution in particular is still very high; a few positive developments were mainly caused by the temporary drop in industrial production. Water pol-

---

30 Cf. Bishop, Gita: Optimism Wanes for a Prompt Cleanup, in: Transition 17 May 1996, pp. 42–45.
31 Cf. Stanners, David/Bourdeau, Philippe (eds.): Europe's Environment. The Dob?í Assessment, Luxembourg 1995.
32 On the previous cooperation of the EU with the CEE states cf.: Gneveckow, Jürgen: Umweltpolitik in Mittel- und Osteuropa – der Prozeß "Umwelt für Europa", in: Osteuropa No. 4, 1996, pp. 343–363.

lution caused by effluents, lacking sewage-treatment plants and overfertilisation of arable land is an equally big problem. Thus the water of the Vistula is so polluted that it cannot even be used for industrial purposes. In disaster areas, as e. g. in Upper Silesia, air and soil pollution by heavy metals have already assumed detrimental proportions, with more and more children suffering genetic damage. Sick rates and mortality rates are further increasing in the ecological crisis areas.

Outmoded nuclear power plants and lacking nuclear security standards are still a great danger – for the West as well. In Bulgaria, Slovakia, the Czech Republic, Slovenia, Hungary and Lithuania, a significant share of electricity (between 40 and 70 percent) is still produced by nuclear power plants of Soviet design. In Lithuania (Ignalina) a nuclear power station of the Chernobyl reactor type is still working. Prolonging the life of these plants, which is supported by western aid programmes, presents a grave risk for Eastern and Western Europe.

According to a World Bank study of 1995, environmental risks have a considerable influence on the investment decisions of foreign enterprises. As payment liabilities for polluted sizes and future emissions continue to be uncertain and information is still lacking, larger investment activities in Central and Eastern Europe are impeded in certain industries. Thus 85 percent of the enterprises interviewed said that they demand relevant information in order to execute environmental analyses at possible investment locations.

Growing crime rates

Since 1989 organised crime and other forms of gangsterism have strongly increased in all post-communist countries. According to estimates, approximately 20 percent of the gross national product in individual Central European states are "earned" in context with organised crime.[33] This development must mainly be seen as a result of the socio-economic upheaval and the opening of the borders, which gave people

---

33 Cf. Heckenberger, Wolfgang: Organisierte Kriminalität – Ein Blick in die Welt, in: Kriminalistik No. 4, 1995, pp. 234–239.

and goods more flexibility to move between east and west. In addition legislation and legal security lag behind the changed economic situation, which gives further leeway for abuse. Moreover, legal ambiguities contribute to massive corruption. To date national and transnational attempts at combating crime have failed. If this development is not stopped, the criminal structures will seriously threaten to destabilise the young democratic societies.

Under these conditions the CEE states might reach for measures which would strictly confine the citizens' basic democratic rights. Given the missing or poorly developed mechanisms of control and security, improper use for political purposes cannot be excluded either.

In some CEE states the present increase in crime is the highest since World War I. Property and white-collar crime as well as drug racketeering have risen alarmingly. Special problem fields are theft, illegal trade with stolen vehicles, weapons and radioactive products as well as traffic in persons. Forms of environmental crime also occur more often, such as e. g. the illegal transport of contaminated waste. If, in particular, border-crossing crime structures increase further, it will become even harder to fight against them in the future. For the CEE states this development bears the risk that reservations and fears in the EU member states towards a speedy eastern enlargement grow.

Lacking reform capacity of the EU

The lacking reform capacity of the EU has become one of the greatest obstacles to the coming eastern enlargement. After being enlarged by ten Central and Eastern European countries plus Malta and Cyprus, a "Community of 27" will no longer be able to work according to rules and methods created for six member states. Reforming the institutions as well as structural and agricultural policy is imperative. The EU's solvency and capacity for action are at stake. While further developing the acquis communautaire of an "EU of 27", differentiating the integration process is inevitable. Otherwise the EU threatens to stagnate in a permanent conflict between the diverging objectives of eastern enlargement and deepening the integration process.

With a view to efficient and democratic decision-making the EU's institutional design has already been overstrained. Eastern enlargement without structurally reforming the EU would result in the Union's being totally overstretched and paralysed. If the present proportional representation was to be retained, a future Commission would consist of more than 30 commissioners. The parliament would be made up of more than 900 representatives. Unanimous decisions in the Council of Ministers would be hard to take as due to the pluralisation of interests the basis for consensus diminishes. In qualified majority decisions the influence of the small states would predominate, with the larger member states' influence on the decision-making process considerably decreasing. In consequence the balance of powers would be fundamentally shifted.

Action is also urgently needed in the field of Common Agricultural Policy (CAP). The number of farmers in the ten associated states is twice as high as in the 15 EU member states together. At present the agricultural output of Central and Eastern Europe makes up approximately 30 percent of the EU's production. Agriculture is still highly important for employment and the generation of income. Through the accession of the ten Central and Eastern European states, the agricultural land of the EU would grow by 44 percent.[34] If the European agricultural policy remained unchanged, the guaranteed prices paid by the EU would provide an incentive to increase production, since the Eastern European agricultural prices presently amount to only 50 to 70 percent of those of the EU. Agricultural production in Central and Eastern Europe would certainly increase. In consequence the European agricultural surplus would grow further and the EU budget would be strained to a much higher extent. If the four so-called "Visegrád states" (Poland, the Czech Republic, Hungary, Slovakia) alone joined the EU in the year 2000, this would cause additional costs of between approximately ECU 5 bn, and up to ten times this amount, unless European agricultural policy were changed.[35]

Reforming the EU's structural policy is equally inevitable. For the

---

[34] Cf. European Commission: Agricultural Situation and Prospects in the Central and Eastern European Countries – Summary Report, Working Document, Brussels 1995.

[35] These prognoses vary considerably depending on the basic assumptions and methods of examination. Cf. the survey in: Brunner, Petra/Ochel, Wolfgang: Die Europäische Union zwischen Vertiefung und Erweiterung, in: ifo Schnelldienst No. 32, 1995, pp. 13ff.

foreseeable future all CEE states will be subject to the presently valid criteria entitling them to support from the EU's structural funds. Even the per capita income of the pacemakers Poland and Hungary is still approximately half of that of the two poorest EU members Greece and Portugal. At present the total national product of the ten associated states does not make up more than 3 percent of that of today's EU.[36] In the next years the growth rates of the Central and Eastern European countries would have to exceed those of the EU by 11 percent in order to reach 50 percent of the EU average by the year 2001 (this was Portugal's level when it entered the EU). However, according to present estimates it is unlikely that the annual growth rate will exceed 5 percent in the medium term. In all probability the CEE states' GDP will make up just about 40 percent of the EU average even by the year 2005. Adhering to the present structural policy would result in burdening the EU with costs which none of the member states would be willing to bear.

Conflicts have already arisen among the 15 member states over the foreseeable redistribution of costs and benefits which the eastern enlargement will entail for the EU.[37] Germany, Austria, Great Britain, Sweden, Finland and Denmark are among those who strongly advocate an eastern enlargement. Germany and Austria, in particular, profit from the growing economic integration of the associated states. Due to the geographical vicinity and economic integration of the Baltic states and Poland, the Scandinavian countries can also count on benefiting from the eastern enlargement. Great Britain, by contrast, hopes that creating a "Europe of 27" will prevent a deepening of the integration process, which might affect national sovereignty. The economically weaker EU states, such as Spain, Italy, Greece, Portugal and Ireland, on the other hand, are afraid of being forced to compete with the CEE states for foreign investment and transfer income after an eastern enlargement. If the 15 member states are unable to reach a compromise, the eastern enlargement could be thwarted by the unanimity rule in the Council of Ministers. Not only would the EU considerably lose credibility in the CEE

---

36 Cf. Tangermann, Stefan: Osterweiterung der EU: Wird die Agrarpolitik zum Hindernis?, in: Wirtschaftsdienst No. 9, 1995, p. 485.
37 Cf. Jung, Christian: Die Osterweiterung und die Interessen der EU-Mitglieder, in: Wirtschaftspolitische Blätter, No. 3–4, 1995, pp. 246–253.

states, but such a failure would also have unpredictable consequences for the cohesion of the present Union.

Unsolved security questions

When the differences of the political systems of East and West were eliminated, the European security order, which was supported by two opposing military alliances, lost its basis. However, to date it has been impossible to create a new all-European security order within the framework of the existing institutions NATO, the Western European Union (WEU) or the EU. If the Euro-Atlantic organisations continued to entrench themselves behind the borders of their alliances and left Central and Eastern Europe to its own devices, new uncalculable security risks would emerge. Remaining within a grey area between "East" and "West" as far as security policy is concerned would, on the one hand, considerably weaken the continuance of internal reforms because they would become prone to different forms of imported instability. On the other hand, Russia is unlikely to constitute a military threat to Central and Eastern Europe at present. However, it cannot be completely excluded for ever. The Baltic states, which in wide sections of Russia are still considered as part of the "near abroad", are particularly concerned. The strong Russian minorities in Latvia and Estonia, open border questions and the future of the enclave in Kaliningrad continue to represent considerable potential sources of conflict.

Meanwhile NATO has started to design the fundament for a new European security system in which NATO itself will assume an important anchor function. NATO faces two main challenges: on the one hand it must react to all CEE states' desire for speedy membership. On the other hand, despite strong Russian misgivings regarding NATO enlargement, it has to create the basis for a new strategic partnership with Russia and the European CIS members.[38] Two misdirected developments within the NATO debate are particularly grave. Firstly, the future eastern enlarge-

---

38 On the discussion about NATO enlargement cf. also: WeltTrends (ed.): NATO Osterweiterung. Neue Mitglieder für ein altes Bündnis?, Berlin 1996.

ments of NATO and the EU are insufficiently coordinated. The decision on a first round of NATO enlargement is likely to be made before talks on EU membership will be entered into, and will probably not be coordinated with them. Secondly, due to a lack of political foresight the worst of all options for a solution threatens to become reality: NATO enlargement will be restricted to some states (Poland, the Czech Republic, Hungary), without a reasonable concept for the remaining states willing to join (the Baltic states in particular), and possibly without a simultaneous security partnership with Russia and Ukraine.

In terms of security policy the biggest problem would thus be the Baltic states, which are exposed to a stronger Russian influence.[39] The geographical vicinity, but above all the large Russian-speaking minorities provide Russia with considerable potential for interference. However, remaining in a state of "Europe in limbo" with respect to security policy would have serious consequences for Slovakia and Bulgaria as well. Both states are characterised by strong ties with Slavic civilisation. Due to traditionally close economic relations Russia is still an important trading partner for them. Until now Bulgaria has been carrying out 60 percent of its foreign trade with the CIS region. Slovakia also remains highly dependent on Russian energy imports, which allows Moscow to retain a considerable degree of influence.

In terms of security policy both countries might feel obliged to reorientate themselves towards Russia. Instead of finding their identity in being firmly anchored in the Euro-Atlantic security structures, Bulgaria and Slovakia could slip into an uncalculable policy of "shifting loyalties", which would result in a considerable amount of instability at the eastern border zones of the future EU.

---

39 For the Baltic issue cf. Asmus, Ronald D. and Nurick, Robert C.: NATO enlargement and the Baltic states, in: Survival, Vol. 38, No. 2, Summer 1996, pp. 121–142.

2. The Balkans

Precarious peace in Bosnia

The Dayton accords between Croatia, the Federal Republic of Yugoslavia (FRY) and Bosnia-Herzegovina have created an extremely fragile edifice of a state. On the one hand they divide the territory of Bosnia-Herzegovina into a Muslim-Croat federation (51 percent) and a Serb republic (49 percent). On the other hand they establish overlapping common institutions for both entities: central government, president, parliament and constitutional court, common currency and central bank. This structure reflects the attitude of the international community that, even though it accepts the territorial results of the war, it nevertheless adheres to the objective of all three ethnic groups living together in one state. Whether the structure of the state worked out in Dayton will ever work in the intended way is still uncertain. Its stability is presently solely based on the presence of the international peace-keeping forces.

Important preconditions for political stability in Bosnia-Herzegovina are missing.[40] Rebuilding residential buildings, factories and public infrastructure alone requires financial means amounting to US$ 5.1 bn for the first three years, which have only partly been financed yet.[41] As many proprietors have fled and not yet returned, property conditions remain unclear, which obstructs urgently needed building projects. An efficient use of available funds cannot be guaranteed. Due to organisational faults relief organisations can use funds only to a limited extent. The local economy is not yet capable of absorbing foreign aid.

Refugees and expellees have not returned to their places of residence because they fear for their safety. The federation's approximately 100 000 Serb inhabitants have left Sarajevo and the federal territory. Most of the Bosnian Muslims (Bosniaks) who have fled do not dare to return to the Serb republic. The troops of the international Stabilisation

---

40 On the situation in Bosnia-Herzegovina cf. e. g. the second progress report of the High Representative for the Implementation of the Peace Agreement on Bosnia-Herzegovina to the UN Secretary-General of 4 July 1996 (UN S/1996/542).
41 Cf. World Bank: Bosnia and Herzegovina. Toward Economic Recovery, Washington 1996.

Force (SFOR) cannot guarantee freedom of movement to the refugees in Bosnia-Herzegovina. In those places within the federation where either Croats or Bosniaks form the majority they obstruct the repatriation of those refugees belonging to the respective minority. In consequence the process of ethnic separation continues. The continuing geographical separation of ethnic groups reinforces ethnical cleavages in politics as it creates ethnically homogeneous blocs and erodes the basis for multi-ethnic organisations and parties in the towns.

In contrast to a relatively successful military implementation of the peace plan, the socio-political reconstruction in Bosnia is not making any progress. The political representatives of the Muslim and Croat population groups refuse on principle to cooperate within the framework of the federation.[42] The Croat side advocates strengthening the confederal ties with the Republic of Croatia. The representatives of the Bosnian Muslims, by contrast, want to maintain the territorial integrity of the federation and favour a more centralised political order. This quarrel could break up the Muslim-Croat federation, the more so since the Party of Democratic Action, currently in power in Bosnia, tends to see itself less and less as a power combining the different ethnic groups. Instead it represents more and more nationalist Islamist positions.

The government of the Bosniak canton around Sarajevo integrated the town as capital of the canton, thus preventing Sarajevo from receiving a special status as national capital. The ethnic make-up of the state administration, the formation of local administrations and the joint federal army are matters of controversy between Bosniaks and Croats. The development of self-governing bodies is not making any progress, neither on the local nor on the cantonal level. Cooperation is particularly problematic in the two cantons with mixed ethnicities. With Mostar being divided into three Bosniak and three Croat town districts and no common central district, the politico-administrative reunification of the Herzegovin regional capital has failed.[43] Organising a joint municipal adminstration was a testcase for the objective to maintain Bosnia-Herzegovina as multi-ethnic state. The EU took over special responsibility for the administration. Ul-

---

42 Frankfurter Allgemeine Zeitung of 10 February 1997.
43 Cf. e. g. Mihalka, Michael: International Failure in Mostar, in: Transition 12 July 1996.

timately, however, it approved of the division instead of the concept of its own administrator. After the EU mandate had expired, violent clashes again occurred between the Croat and Bosniak inhabitants.

If the federation as the heart of a new body politic fails, it will become even harder to launch a cooperation between the parts of the Republic of Bosnia-Herzegovina – the Croat-Muslim federation and the Serb republic. After the conclusion of the Dayton accords the Serb leader Karadzic, who is prosecuted as a war criminal, and his followers tried to obstruct all beginnings of cooperation. They have been given considerable potential for interference by the rigid schedule set for implementing the civil parts of the agreement and the limited authority of the High Representative for Yugoslavia, Carl Bildt. Much depends on whether moderate Serb politicians take over leadership within the Serb ethnic group, and on how attractive the leadership of the Serb republic considers the alternative of joining the FRY. If, however, nationalist politicians were able to stand their ground, the Serb republic would do everything to prevent joint-state institutions in Bosnia-Herzegovina from working. The situation would then certainly escalate, which would make it impossible to bring political peace to the country.

Security risks of a disintegration of Bosnia

Whether Bosnia-Herzegovina can be reconstructed as a state, to a great extent depends on which policy will be pursued by the FRY and Croatia, which also signed the Dayton agreement. By signing the peace accords the FRY also acknowledged Bosnia-Herzegovina as independent state and formally renounced uniting all Serbs in one state. Since Milosevic's government advocated the conclusion of peace, the Bosnian Serbs' confidence in its patronage is shaken. Croatia's policy is ambivalent insofar as, on the one hand, it acknowledged Bosnia-Herzegovina early on and supported the implementation of the political aims of Dayton. On the other hand, Croatia considers the Bosnian-Herzegovin Croats its own citizens. The Bosnian-Herzegovin Croats could, for example, take part in the Croat elections of October 1995. There is some danger that more or less openly declared alliances between Serb and Croat minorities and their respective patronage states might be formed after the withdrawal of the international forces. These coalitions of interest will further intensify the influence Croatia and the FRY exert on Bosnia-Herzegovina, thus aiming at a secession of the Serb republic or the Croat cantons respectively.[44] If the Croat and Serb territories joined Croatia, or the FRY and Bosnia-Herzegovina disintegrated, the question of what would become of the settlement areas of the Bosnian Muslims would remain open. For geographical, economic and political reasons the establishment of an independent Bosniak skeleton state is extremely problematic. In all probability such a state would become increasingly dependent on Croatia or the FRY. If Bosnia-Herzegovina disintegrated, the international community would be faced with a dilemma:

- The international community can either accept the division of the Bosniak territories between Croatia and the FRY. In this case the Bosniaks would offer fierce military resistance. However, sooner or later they would have to surrender to the superior strength of the Croats and Serbs. New waves of refugees, "ethnic cleansing campaigns" and political oppression would be the consequences. The UN, NATO and the EU would be highly discredited in the Balkan region and the Islamic countries. A precedent would be created for how to violate borders successfully by force, which would have an impact for the rest of the Balkans and other world regions.
- Alternatively the international community defends the territorial integrity of an autonomous Bosniak state. However, the experience made in the war in former Yugoslavia support the asssumption that a mere arms and trade embargo does not offer an effective protection against aggressors. From the very beginning the international community would have to reconsider the option of more efficient military means.

In principle it would be possible to equip the Bosniaks financially and militarily already in the run-up to a war, thus producing military parity in the region. Whether, with a view to the strategic vulnerability of a Bosniak state, this would after all be feasible is, however, questionable.

---

44 Cf. Calic, Marie-Janine: Das Abkommen von Dayton. Chancen und Risiken des Friedensprozesses im ehemaligen Jugoslawien. SWP AP 2948, Ebenhausen March 1996.

This question would probably bring the smouldering quarrel between the EU and the USA to a head and further strain transatlantic relations. Whereas the EU foreign ministers have kept up the arms embargo on the successor states of the former Yugoslavia (with the exceptions of Macedonia and Slovenia) to date, the USA have supported the training and armament of the Bosnian-Herzegovin army and have made funds amounting to US$ 100 m available for this purpose.[45] Thus the USA counteract efforts of the OSCE to come to an agreement on armament control and disarmament with Croatia, Bosnia-Herzegovina and the FRY. If military parity could not be established to form a convincing deterrent, a new violent conflict in the region would, however, mainly affect Europe, which would have to carry the costs for the American strategy.

A policy backing regional military parity and a Bosniak state capable of defending itself will have problems of credibility. These will confront the international community with the decision of whether again to commit itself militarily in order to keep up this state's integrity. If Bosnia-Herzegovina disintegrated, defending the territorial integrity of a Bosniak skeleton state would also require UN or NATO military commitment (which both organisations threatened convincingly). Russia is an uncertain factor in this scenario. Domestic politics or geostrategic interests could motivate a Russian leadership once again, and this time more intensely, to act as protecting power for the Serbs or refuse to accept NATO intervention. At any rate, a permanent security guarantee with military reinforcement would require immense expenditure. However, the costs of another violent confrontation would be much higher.

Potential conflicts in the southern Balkans

A series of conflicts in the southern Balkans is so charged with ethnic interests and patterns of thinking that there is hardly any room for rational political settlement. The situation is particularly tense in the Serbian province of Kosovo. For years ethnic Albanians, who make up 90 percent of

---

45 Cf. Common Position of the EU Council of Foreign Ministers of 26 February 1996, in: Agence Europe of 27 March 1996; Süddeutsche Zeitung of 16/17 March 1996; Woodard, Colin: Buildung Up Bosnia's Army, in: Transition 1 November 1996.

the population in this region, have opposed Serbia, which has claimed Kosovo as the cradle of the Serb nation. The Serb government has proclaimed martial law for the region. It represses political manifestations of the Albanian shadow state and applies all forms of oppression against the Albanian citizens. The Kosovo Albanians strive for an independent Republic of Kosovo under international protection. In addition, they demand from the international community not to discontinue economic sanctions against Serbia unless Serb behaviour in Kosovo is changed. The Albanians want to enter into negotiations under the mediation of the UN, the EU or other international organisations. The Serb government, by contrast, is willing to enter into negotiations on Kosovo, but considers the status of the province an internal Serb problem. Attacks against Serbs and statements by leading Albanian officials about an "Intifada" along the Palestinian pattern show that the Albanians are ceasing to support non-violent action. The risk of violent confrontation is increasing.[46]

The "Albanian question"[47] might also be raised by nationalist forces in neighbouring Albania, which, in view of the economic and social tensions in Albania, could gain influence. The Albanian government has been the only foreign government to acknowledge the Kosovo Albanians' shadow state. Furthermore it supports the Macedonian Albanians' demand for autonomy. It was merely due to western pressure that the Albanian government was willing to act in a more reserved manner in the minority question. Albania now obviously backs a multilateral settlement of the minority problem instead of directly lobbying particular interests. To date, the situation of the Albanian minorities has not been settled sactisfactorily, neither within the neighbour states nor between Albania and its neighbours. If Albania tried to reunite the minorities living in Kosovo, the Former Yugoslav Republic of Macedonia (Macedonia) and Greece with the mother country, this would provoke a conflict in the southern Balkans which would be as dangerous as the Serb nationalism in the former Yugoslavia.

---

46 Cf. Rubin, Barnett R. (ed.): Toward Comprehensive Peace in Southeast Europe. Conflict Prevention in the South Balkans, New York 1996.
47 Cf. Troebst, Stefan: The "Albanian Question", in: Marie-Janine Calic (ed.): Friedenskonsolidierung im ehemaligen Jugoslawien: Sicherheitspolitische und zivile Aufgaben, SWP S 413, Ebenhausen 1996.

In Macedonia the delicate domestic consensus between the governing party alliance for Macedonia and its Albanian coalition partner threatens to break. With parties representing the ethnic Albanians allowed to participate in the government, a first step has bee taken to divide power between the population groups. In principle the Macedonian government is willing to give the Albanian minority a proportional share in all state institutions. However, it refuses to accept the Albanian claim to acknowledge them constitutionally as state nation. Radical positions seem to gain influence within the Albanian colony: following a police operation against the opening of an Albanian-speaking university in the Tetovo region in April 1995, a radical wing separated from the Albanian party. This group aims at founding a separate state. In October 1995 extremists attempted to assassinate the Macedonian President Gligorov, who strove for an integration of the Albanians. If violence in Kosovo escalates, it could easily spread to the Albanian colony in Macedonia and result in an internal destabilisation of the Macedonian state.

With the establishment of a broad Albanian secessionist movement withdrawing loyalty from the Macedonian state, the neighbour states could find cause to question the sovereignty of Macedonia. Albania would probably act as protecting power to "its own" countrymen. Even though the FRY and Bulgaria acknowledged Macedonia, they could, however, in case of a radicalisation claim Macedonia's Christian-Orthodox, Slav population as part of the Serb and Bulgarian nation. In a bilateral interim agreement (September 1995) Greece and Macedonia may well have settled their quarrels about the Macedonian constitution and state symbols and declared the inviolability of their borders. (In consequence Greece lifted its trade embargo.) However, the name of the republic is still disputed, and in Greece the name "Macedonia" is still perceived as an irredentist threat.[48]

The respective minorities continue to cause problems in the relations between Greece and Albania. The Greek minority in southern Albania demands that the network of educational institutions and opportunities be enlarged. The living conditions of the Albanian labour migrants in Greece

---

48 Perry, Duncan M.: On the Road to Stability – or Destruction?, in: Transition 25 August 1995, and Troebst, Stefan: Macedonia – Powder Keg Defused?, in: RFE/RL Research Report 28 January 1994.

are problematic mainly because of their illegal status. Since a radical Greek "Liberation Front Northern Epirus" attacked an Albanian military base in April 1994, relations between both countries have deteriorated. It took the foreign ministers till March 1995 to agree on several steps towards normalising the situation.[49] Afterwards Greece started to legalise the status of the Albanian labour migrants and to support Albania's integration into European structures. Albania, for its part, will allow private schools in the minority territory, enlarge the educational system for the minority and reduce Greek businessmen's obligation to hold a visa.

In addition, as a reaction to a disintegration of Bosnia-Herzegovina and an isolation of the Bosnian Muslims, an Islamist movement could develop to form a coalition between the Muslims in Bosnia-Herzegovina, Sandzak and Albania. For quite some time close contacts have existed between the Bosnian government party and the party of the Sandzak-Muslims. In recent years Islam has gained influence in all three regions. Thus, a front between the Christian-Orthodox countries Greece, Bulgaria and Serbia and a new Islamic "axis" from Turkey to Iran could develop, continuing the permanent Greek-Turkish conflict.[50] Although this scenario seems to reflect an inclination towards geopolitical thinking, radicalisation and the strengthening of fundamentalist forces in the region are well conceivable.

Underdevelopment and political destabilisation

Today the question of whether, and when, the Balkan region will be able to catch up economically with states such as the Czech Republic, Hungary or Slovenia is still open. It is equally uncertain whether the Balkans will move further away from the other states and develop typical characteristics of a "poor capitalism". Croatia is the only Balkan country where preconditions for economic modernisation are favourable.[51] The pros-

---

49 Reuter, Jürgen: Athens schwieriger Weg zum Abschluß eines Interim-Abkommens mit Skopje, in: Südosteuropa-Mitteilungen Vol. 35, No. 4, 1995, pp. 333–359.
50 Glenny, Misha: Heading off War in the Southern Balcans, in: Foreign Affairs, May-June 1995.
51 Cf. Deutsche Bank Research (ed.): Osteuropa-Themen: Kroatien No. 165, 28 October 1996; Frankfurter Allgemeine Zeitung of 15 April and 2 May 1996.

pects for overcoming historical differences in the development of Central and Eastern Europe and the Balkans have rather worsened, the more so since attempts at reducing regional differences within the former Yugoslavia have failed. During the transformation period since 1990/91, though, Albania has managed very quickly to develop and reduce the distance to the backward regions of the former Yugoslavia. However, in all Balkan societies traditional modes of behaviour, patterns of thinking and structures have proved to persist which the communist system had either partly hidden or even generated itself. In the Balkan region democracy and market economy remain fragile constructions, which have not yet been firmly anchored in social relations until now.

In addition many social and economic problems of the transformation have not been solved in the Balkan countries. The states lack foreign capital in order to modernise industrial structures. At the same time they depend more and more on foreign financial aid, and foreign debt increases. In many sectors the transformation process has come to a halt, among other reasons because enterprises have run up debts in order to evade the tight budget restrictions introduced in the course of stabilisation. The interdependence of economic actors promotes clientelist loyalties and networks. A local middle class has not yet developed. At the same time income differentiation is growing, but income is not distributed according to performance.

Similar to other European transformation states, a small group of profiteers, flaunting a life-style of western luxury, has emerged in the Balkans. At the lower end, by contrast, a new class of people losing out against transformation has developed, who have been socially and economically degraded. These population groups can be mobilised to a particularly high degree by ethnic differences. Moreover they will continue to surge into Western Europe's illegal labour markets in order to escape from their situation, which offers them no prospects at all. Colonies of Southeast European immigrants in countries such as Germany threaten to be followed by more and more waves of labour migrants.

The continuing economic underdevelopment closely interacts with permanent political instability. Party pluralism is less developed than in the Central and Eastern European states, and there are tendencies towards an authoritarian, Latin-American style of corporatism. Party systems are only loosely anchored in societal groups. The contrasts between individual parties often merely reflect conflicts between different groups of the élite or intelligentsia or just personal animosities. Since the Croat Democratic Union or the Socialist Party of Serbia are mainly elected by older, less qualified and rural parts of the population – the potential losers of the economic transformation –, these parties will always be susceptible to patterns of populist and nationalist policies. Even parties such as Tudjman's Croat Democratic Union or the Democratic Party in Serbia, which present themselves as "civil" parties, take up populist positions. Thus the political process is likely to waver between right-wing or left-wing populism and technocratic professionalism.[52] Civil-liberal parties have only little influence. It is still uncertain whether the Serbian opposition coalition Zajedno will provide a convincing alternative to Milosevic's régime.

For most Balkan governments the constitutional state is an instrument to excercise political power. They try to bring all decision-making authority under their central control and subverts any attempts at a division of powers. Thus the Croat government systematically obstructs the election of oppositional mayors. The Serb government refused to give in to the demands for democratic reforms voiced by the movement of the opposition parties and the students. It stubbornly resisted the campaign for the recognition of the results of the local elections.[53] In Serbia, in particular, but also in Albania and the other countries of the region, the governing élites frequently ignore the autonomy of the judiciary and the media. Within the FRY the balance of power between the constituent republics of Montenegro and Serbia remains unstable since the Montenegran government is confronted by an opposition which wants to enlarge the republic's autonomy. The constitutional status of the former autonomous provinces of Vojvodina and Kosovo with their ethnic Hungarian and Albanian populations has not been clarified. As a result of arbitrary and centralist rule, different interests are further charged with ethnic contents. These tendencies counteract the development of a democratic political culture. They make politics more unpredictable and

---

52 Cf. Przeworski, Adam (ed.): Sustainable Democracy, Cambridge 1996.
53 Cf. e. g. Frankfurter Allgemeine Zeitung of 6 February 1997.

offer a breeding ground for authoritarian-populist forces. Thus political tensions within the Balkan countries could intensify and erupt into internal and external violence.

3. Russia and the CIS

Disintegration or reintegration

Six years after the collapse of the USSR the future of the post-Soviet space has become more uncertain than ever. Contrary to initial hopes the Commonwealth of Independent States (CIS) has not become a guarantee for stability and security. The development is characterised by profound contradictions, which are intensified by Russian hegemonic demands. The emerging alliance between Russia, Belarus and Kazakhstan remains fragile. For a "Slav Union" Ukraine is missing; for a veritable "Eurasian Union" the other Central Asian republics were needed. Moreover the integration of Transcaucasus is uncertain. Meanwhile a series of old and new conflict factors threaten the union's coherence – with far-reaching consequences also for the West:
- the principal asymmetry of mutual interests. Russia is, in the first place, striving for an alliance in terms of security and military policy. The other states, by contrast, are in the short run looking for economic advantages in order to achieve their long-term aim of national stabilisation.
- the competition for existing raw material deposits, mainly in the Caspian Sea. Moscow's pressure on Azerbaijan shows a tendency towards not respecting the sovereignty of other CIS republics. In view of the high priority of CIS policy, the danger of a new "CIS doctrine" of limited sovereignty threatens to increase.
- the persistently volatile status of the Russian minorities in the neighbour republics. The presence of more than 20 million Russians in the so-called "near abroad" gives Moscow considerable potential for interference. Moscow has clearly pointed out that it reserves itself the

option to defend the interest of the minorities by use of force, if necessary.
– continuous national-ethnic conflicts within the CIS, mainly in Tajikistan, Georgia (Abkhasia, South-Ossetia) and Armenia/Azerbaijan (Nagorno-Karabakh). The presence of Russian armed forces (130 000 troops on non-Russian territory of the CIS[54]) has managed temporarily to pacify the conflicts. In no way, however, have they been settled. On the contrary, Russia is interested in keeping the conflicts simmering in order to warrant its own status as ordering power. Russia's double dealing threatens to prolong the confrontations and make it impossible to bring stable and long-term peace to the CIS region.

The presidential elections in 1996 showed that elections in Russia cannot be won by way of openly restorative rhetorics. Nevertheless the CIS policy continues to have top priority in foreign policy.[55] Since the CIS debate might still be connected with the question of NATO's eastern enlargement, an escalation of the situation remains possible: Moscow threatened to instrumentalise the argument about NATO enlargement in order to push forward the Russian integration policy in the CIS. The danger of an aggressive Russian CIS policy would quickly put a sharper edge to the NATO debate. Possible scenarios for a new East-West confrontation are more easily conceivable on the territory of the former USSR than elsewhere. Apart from a forced reunification with Belarus, three potential crisis areas would directly affect western interests if the situation aggravated:

Ukraine

Ukraine remains Russia's most important neighbour state. Until today its independence has hardly been accepted by the political class. The closer union with Belarus gives fresh impetus to the dream of a "Slav Union".

---

54 Blackwill, Robert D. et al.: Engaging Russia. A Report to the Trilateral Commission, Triangle Paper No. 46, p. 9.
55 For a new note in the debate cf. Kortunov, Andrej: Zwischen Imperium und Weltharmonie, in: Internationale Politik No. 1 1997, pp. 9–14. The author argues for a new strategy of selective commitment for Russia.

Russia openly distrusts the active commitment of the USA and Germany in Ukraine. Even though Moscow can hardly be keen on an open destabilisation of Ukraine, Russian and western interests in Ukraine oppose each other in the long term. A few alarming factors give reason to fear that Ukraine could become the scene of a new "Cold Peace" (B. Yeltsin) between East and West: the stagnating reform course and the continuous political and economic instability of Ukraine; secondly the growing power of influential – not only national-patriotic – forces in Russia, which try to make Ukraine join the "union treaty" with Belarus and Kazakhstan[56]; and thirdly the potential, still unsettled conflicts between Russia and Ukraine, which gain additional explosive power from the sovereignty clauses in the new Ukrainian constitution. As long as the long-expected bilateral treaty of friendship is not signed, the numerous disputed questions (Sebastopol, Black Sea Fleet, Crimea, Russian minorities in eastern Ukraine, power supplies, Ukrainian indebtedness) can always be instrumentalised in favour of a confrontation.

The Caspian Sea

The most explosive future conflict could be caused by the exploitation of energy resources and pipeline structures at the Caspian Sea.[57] In 1995/6 the quarrel over the "project of the century", i. e. the exploitation of Caspian oil fields, and future pipeline routes was finally settled by acceptable compromises. However, the international struggle for the Kazakh oil deposits, which are more important by far, has just begun. Massive and long-term interests are at stake for all international parties (Russia, USA, Turkey, Iran). To date a cooperative and pragmatic policy has dominated in Moscow. However, the still influential national-authoritarian forces in Moscow could insist on a harder line to secure Russian interest

---

56 Thus a study of the Russian Council of Foreign and Defence Policy, entitled "Will the (Soviet) Union revive by 2005?", propagates an active strategy of reintegration towards Ukraine. Cf. Jamestown Foundation (ed.): Jamestown Prism Vol. 2, No. 12, Part 4 1996.
57 Rahr, Alexander: Die Sicherung der Energietransportwege. Eine strategische Aufgabe für Rußland, in: Internationale Politik No. 1 1997, pp. 25–30; Forsythe, Rosemary: The Politics of Oil in the Caucasus and Central Asia, in: Institute for International and Strategic Studies (ed.): Adelphi Papers No. 300, London 1996.

in the Caspian Sea. Given the vital western interests in energy policy, the region could quickly become the focal area of a new conflict with Russia.

Russian minorities in the CIS republics

With CIS policy given high priority in Russian foreign policy, the danger of instrumentalising the minority issue has increased. The danger of escalation is particularly high in those CIS republics in which the Russian population groups, quietly or openly, show separatist tendencies (Moldavia, Crimea, Kazakhstan). Such a development could be fuelled if the economic development, in Ukraine in particular, fell further behind. New waves of refugees and expellees would further destabilise the whole region. The new Russian military doctrine explicitly lays down the conditions subject to which Russia feels entitled to intervene in the "near abroad". In contrast to the war in Chechnya, every open conflict between Russia and a CIS neighbour state would not be a "Russian domestic issue" and put the future partnership with Russia to a hard test.

Slow democratisation

The main question facing an enlarged European Union is how relations with the future eastern neighbour states Russia, Belarus, Ukraine and, in the long term, also Moldavia will develop. The internal change continues to be unstable in all four European CIS republics. The political development is unpredictable, mainly in Belarus, but also in Russia. On the one hand, social pluralisation has become more dynamic than could have been expected at the end of the 1980s. Regular elections have taken place; several new actors and lobbies have been consolidated; and a critical media landscape has asserted itself. These signs indicate that democratic processes are being reinforced. With its first free presidential elections since 1991 Russia has passed an impressive democratic test. The danger of a communist return seems to be banned even in Russia.

Nevertheless, democracy is not safe in any of the future eastern EU neighbour states. In none of the three countries does a stable legal and institutional framework guarantee that the democratic development remains irreversible. In Belarus, in particular, authoritarian and antidemocratic tendencies are moving towards a dictatorship under President Lukashenko. In Russia, a return towards the principle of strong "state power" (derzhavnost), to which civil rights and freedoms are subordinated, is obvious. Whereas in the period of *Glasnost* under Gorbachev progress was made with a view to democratisation, regress has taken place under President Yeltsin.[58] Yeltsin did not win the presidential elections as a democratic reformer, but as an authoritarian power politician, who stressed Russia's national interests. The danger of an autocratic régime, not firmly anchored in the population, has not yet been banned forever in any of the western CIS republics.

Social misery and crisis represent the biggest potential danger in all CIS countries. Even in the westernmost CIS states the gulf between losers and "*nouveaux riches*", mainly affecting the old educated élites, runs much deeper than in Central and Eastern Europe. More than half of the population in all three states has become destitute, with a third living below subsistence level.[59] The deterioration of the health system is accompanied by an alarming demographic development. Despite a slight stabilisation, the average life expectancy has fallen below all European standards (Russia 1990: 65 years for men, today just under 57 years).[60] In addition, unemployment, which in view of the retarded reforms is just about to hit, is growing. For wide circles of the population the prevailing pauperisation has seriously undermined the credibility of democratic and economic reforms. For many people the terms "reform" and "democracy" have been discredited and become synonyms of a "criminal revolution". Whether the economic and social needs of these (mainly rural) parts of the population can be fulfilled in the foreseeable future is questionable. Meanwhile this disillusionment is a threat to the further

---

58 Cf. Deutsch-Russischer Austausch et al.: Zur Situation der Menschen- und Bürgerrechte in Rußland. Materialien und Aufsätze, Berlin 1996. Cf. also Report of the Human Rights Commission under the chairmanship of Sergei Kovalyov, documented in Frankfurter Rundschau of 13/14 September 1994.
59 Cf. results of a seminar organised by the Friedrich-Ebert-Foundation on the "Phenomenon of poverty in contemporary Russia", Frankfurter Allgemeine Zeitung of 20 October 1995; cf. also Penny, Morvant: The Changing Face of Poverty, in: Transition 12 January 1996.
60 Penny, Morvant: Alarm over Falling Life Expectancy, in: Transition 20 October 1995.

success of the transformation of the system and harbours the danger of serious destabilisation. Different risk scenarios could become real:

Restorative tendencies threaten to increase mainly in Belarus. After the referendum of last November, the country is moving towards a dictatorship under President Lukashenko and an even closer dependence on Russia. In Ukraine, by contrast, inner conflicts, instability and chaos remain the biggest risks. Tensions in the eastern parts of the country would be most reinforced if the economy fell further back behind Russia. Ukraine's national identity has visibly been consolidated within the last years. Nevertheless – more than in all other transformation states – economic disintegration and social misery threaten the existence of the Ukrainian state as such.

Neither can a return to authoritarian rule be fully excluded in Russia. A clear division of powers (i. e. mainly a functioning rule of law) is missing; decision-making processes are not transparent (influence of the Security Council and the increasingly powerful financial oligarchy, clans around the presidential apparatus). At the same time the security services continue to exert an unclear influence. A creeping departure from the processes of democratic development still seems possible. Alarming signals are: the concentration of power in the hands of the president and the new "oligarchy of power"; continuous governing "by decree" while simultaneously ignoring the new constitution; and the permanent weakness of the parliament. The human rights policy continues to be characterised by severe deficits.

Human rights activist Sergei Kovalyov's warnings of a "police state Russia" are certainly exaggerated. Neither does pilloring Yeltsin's Russia as a persistently "communist system of governance under anti-communist slogans"[61] do justice to the historical changes since 1991. However, the danger that Russia's constitutional principles (law) could again be subordinated to the state's ordering power (order) is not perceived as a threat, but finds considerable backing in the population. The majority of the population clearly reject the return to communist structures and restriction of political freedoms; however, at the same time the model of

---

61 Sergei Kovalyov, quoted in Financial Times of 15/16 June 1996, as well as the analysis of the reputed historian Yuri Afanasyev, Die Tageszeitung of 18 June 1996.

western democracies has found increasingly less support since 1991.[62] In Belarus and Russia at least, unlike most Central and Eastern European states, the yearning for a "firm-hand" policy seems to be stronger than the desire for further democratisation.

The connection of authoritarian tendencies with nationalist-xenophobic trends in Russia still remains a long-term danger. Even though the communists were unable to assert themselves with their nationalistically tinged collectivism, the population lives on in a "double" nostalgia based on old traditions of the Russian Empire and the Soviet era. The lack of a culture built on making compromises as a basis for a peaceful internal balance of interests is a legacy of this double past. Contrary to Central and Eastern Europe, the use of force has temporarily been re-established as political instrument in Russia – as early as in 1993 with the shelling of the parliamentary building, mostly, however, with the war in Chechnya. If public order further deteriorates and extremist groups continue to proliferate, the danger of social polarisation and readiness for using force will increase. Such a development could lead to internal authoritarianism and external isolation and xenophobia. This could, in turn, easily develop into confrontation. Partnership and cooperation would be impossible with a nationalist-aggressive Russia. An authoritarian Russia, however, would also be a more than troublesome partner for Europe.

Economic setbacks

The key to the future of the eventual eastern neighbours of the EU is their permanent macroeconomic stabilisation. Despite a few positive tendencies (stabilisation of the inflation rate, normalisation of the budget legislation etc.), the transformation-induced recession has not been overcome to date in any of the states of the former Soviet Union. In the foreseeable future economic normalisation seems to be out of sight. The core problem of each transformation state, i. e. finding a balance between restructuring and stabilisation, seems to be almost insoluble in the successor republics of the Soviet Union. It remains unclear in all countries how the

---

62 Cf. European Commission: Eurobarometer Survey, Brussels 1994.

conflict between strict monetary policy and the necessary increase in social expenditure can be settled.

A dynamically growing private sector, mainly in the service industries, is an important bearer of hope for the CIS reform states, too. According to conservative estimates the non-state sector (comprising private enterprises and those with state participation) meanwhile accounts for a third of the GDP generated in Russia[63] (i. e. it only slowly approximates the level of the CEE states, though statistics remain highly unreliable). In Ukraine the development of the private sector lags behind considerably. Only half as many units as in Russia have yet been privatised; in Belarus the share of the private sector is one of the lowest in the whole CIS – even according to optimistic estimates it does not make up more than 17 percent.[64] In all three countries obstacles to a healthy development of the private sector are still enormous. To start with, the banking sector is instable; emerging capital markets are weak; and legal uncertainty persists. Moreover, crime and corruption threaten the development of a new corporate culture.[65] As long as framework conditions for a favourable investment climate do not improve, the future of the private sector will not be guaranteed in any of these states.

Up to now nothing has been able to stop the serious investment crisis which is the biggest obstacle on the way towards stable economic growth in the CIS states.[66] Reluctance to invest is the key problem to stand in the way of economic recovery; no increase can be expected before 1997. Even foreign investment, which in 1995 for the first time considerably increased in Russia, lags far behind that in the Central and Eastern European states.[67] In Russia, in particular, the persistent capital flight, the continuous real revaluation of the rouble and the stagnating agricultural policy

---

63 Havlik, Peter: ibd., p. 31.
64 Boss, Helen: Ukraine: better, but not good enough, in Podkaminer et. al.: ibd., pp. 103–109. For a more optimistic evaluation cf. also Frankfurter Allgemeine Zeitung GmbH Informationsdienste (ed.): Länderanalysen Ukraine/Weißrußland, April 1996 and World Bank: ibd., p. 15.
65 According to a recent study of the Russian interior ministry, up to 40 percent of GDP is now made up by the so-called "shadow economy". The economic crime rate rose by 12.5 per cent from 1995 to 1996, cf. Frankfurter Allgemeine Zeitung of 11 February 1997.
66 Institut für Weltwirtschaft (ed.): Die wirtschaftliche Lage Rußlands: Investitionsschwäche verhindert Wachstum; as well as Deutsches Institut für Wirtschaftsforschung (ed.): Die wirtschaftliche Lage der Republik Belarus, in: Wochenbericht No. 19, 1996, pp. 328–337.
67 For a comparative survey of the cumulative direct foreign investment in Central and Eastern Europe and the CIS cf. World Bank: ibd., p. 64.

impede growth. Real incomes have further decreased in Russia, Belarus and Ukraine in 1996. The West must expect a continuing scenario of stable depression before a – not yet foreseeable – upturn in all three states.

The relapse into planned-economy thinking is another danger. The continuous influence of old monopolist structures and the power of a new "finance nomenclature" remains a basic evil of post-Soviet economies. The newly established "Financial Industrial Groups" (FIGs), of which 100 were already supposed to be created by 1997, could form an obstacle to a liberalisation of the economy.[68] In the three European CIS states, parliaments hostile to reforms continue to obstruct the legislation necessary for a structural change. Stagnation in the privatisation process and tendencies towards a return to subsidised industrial policy and protectionism also remain causes for concern. Despite supporting continuing reforms, the Russian leadership has also backed customs barriers and stronger state control over important industrial branches.[69] Belarus' confrontation course has already angered the international financial institutions.[70] Much is at stake for Russia, but also for Ukraine and Belarus. Economic growth, which is needed in order to overcome the recession caused by the transformation, could further be obstructed. In the long term the countries run the risk that the inflow of western capital and know-how, which is meagre anyway, will come to a standstill. More important, however, is that if reforms were retarded, support given by the international finance institutions would be stopped. At present none of the CIS economies can survive without them.

The possible disconnection of the economic reform course from a simultaneous liberalisation of society also harbours risks. Social misery and disillusionment of the population are accompanied by a growing rejection of the liberal western social model and could accelerate such a trend. Thus wide sections of the political élite in Russia consider China and Chile as blueprints for a successful reform economy under central state control. By drifting towards a "regulated market economy without democracy", Russia would be disconnected from all-European values.

---

68 For a comprehensive survey cf. Hofheinz, Paul: The Big Fig, in: Russia Review Vol. 3, No. 89, 1996, pp. 1,8–13.
69 Handelsblatt of 6 March 1996 and Süddeutsche Zeitung of 2 July 1996.
70 Neue Zürcher Zeitung of 29 June 1996.

The European partners would be confronted with a new and difficult form of neighbourhood.

Another set of problems results from the development of foreign trade. The radical reorientation of trade towards the West is a trend-setting success of the reform states' adjustment. With the EFTA states joining the EU, the importance of the EU for Russia, Ukraine and Belarus has further increased. The future eastern enlargement will reinforce the trend towards integration in terms of trade policy.[71] Even though anti-western rhetoric is on the increase, the economic development of the countries depends more and more on cooperation with the West. Yet negative tendencies are spreading. Thus German-Russian trade, a traditionally important indicator, shows clear signs of stagnation. In 1995 Russia, which had always been the biggest eastern partner of German economy, was, for the first time, relegated to second place by Poland.[72]

Integrating the post-Soviet economies into world economics remains the most difficult challenge. Russia is a warning example for the other republics. On the one hand, it is the only eastern transformation country continuously to achieve trade surpluses with the western industrial states. On the other hand, even Russia has not succeeded in playing a role in international trade which would go beyond that of a raw material supplier.[73] In addition, the expansion of Russian exports in the raw material sector threatens to reach its limits. In 1995 Russian power production decreased by 3 percent on average; to date the crisis in power production has not been stopped. Moreover it would be necessary to diversify the export structure. This is, however, opposed by the continuous "primitivisation" of Russian industrial production.[74] Without strengthening the

---

71 Clement, Hermann: ibd., pp. 46–53. On Ukraine's growing EU trade cf. Neue Zürcher Zeitung of 10 May 1996.
72 Cf. Wartenberg von, Ludolph: Chancen und Perspektiven für die deutsche Industrie in Mittel- und Osteuropa, paper given on the occasion of the conference "Transformation in Eastern Europe: present developments and future trends and chances for cooperation with economy" in Berlin on 20/21 June 1996.
73 Institut für Weltwirtschaft et al. (ed.): Die wirtschaftliche Lage Rußlands. Rußland in der Weltwirtschaft: Noch nicht mehr als ein Exporteur von Rohstoffen. Siebenter Bericht, Teil II, Kieler Diskussionsbeiträge 265, Kiel 1996.
74 Cf. Documentation of the Bundesstelle für Außenhandelsinformation (BfAI; Federal Office for Foreign Trade Information) for the Second Economic Conference on Russia on 27 March 1996, p. 19. On Russia's foreign trade structure cf. also Clement, Hermann: ibd., p. 53, and Havlik, Peter: ibd., p. 32. According to these sources machinery and equipment make up only 6.8 percent (1995) of Russian exports.

manufacturing industry, Russian industrial exports do not stand a chance in foreign markets. If the export capacity of the Russian economy decreases, this does not only put Russia's integration into the G 7 at stake, but also its future as international economic power.

Russia as unpredictable super-power

Since 1993 a growing consensus on a more independent course in foreign policy has established itself in Russia.[75] All political camps aim at Russia's recognition as international super-power with acknowledged areas of influence. As this development has been the first and only factor in post-Soviet Russia to create a consensus, it is of great importance. The new agenda rejects closer relations with the West as "romanticism" of the late 1980s and determinedly pursues its objective of realising Russian "national interests" as part of a traditional super-power policy. However, national interests have not completely been defined. While the new financial oligarchy clearly seeks to strengthen Russia's power through economic cooperation with the West, Russia has not yet finally declared where it wants to find its new position between the CIS, Europe, rivalry with the USA and the up-and-coming Asian-Pacific neighbours. The lessons of the late Soviet era, which made an opening towards the western community seem advisable to the country, threaten to fall into oblivion. Instead of stressing global interdependence, the "old way of thinking" is given political priority, and Russia insists on its super-power status. Contrary to the Federal Republic of Germany, which after the collapse of 1945 concentrated on integration and "forgetting about power", a scenario of isolation and "obsession with power" is looming in Russia.

The lack of political, economic and military resources to enforce an effective super-power policy complicates the situation even further. Western experts assume that even in the medium term Russia will not be able to bridge the gap between super-power pretensions and reality.[76]

---

75 Cf. Timmermann, Heinz: Präsidentschaftswahlen in Rußland: Grundlinien und Perspektiven der Außen- und Sicherheitspolitik, in: Aktuelle Analysen des BIOst No. 31, 1996.
76 On the discussion about the resources of Russian foreign policy cf. Vogel, Heinrich: Rußland als Partner der europäischen Politik, in: Berichte des BIOst No. 8, 1996, pp. 24 ff.

Russia can at best obtain regional dominance within the CIS. Yet, it is the compensatory function of a neo-imperialist and confrontative foreign policy which creates great uncertainty and unpredictability. Thus, for the West the question of how to deal with a Russia which openly violates western interests and values (inter alia towards third states, such as Iran, Iraq and China) gains more importance. Two negative scenarios seem possible:

Russia in isolation

Russia is not in danger of becoming isolated, but of isolating itself. Dangerous tendencies are the revival of the old myth of a "separate way" for Russia and the growing rejection of international dependencies. Isolationist forces are given impetus by the uncertainty about the Russian identity after the collapse of the Soviet Union. Gradually, national strength is again defined along the lines of the old geostrategic patterns of the 19th century (territory, military power). The new notion that political influence is considerably determined by economic power and the capacity for innovation still has to assert itself beyond the narrow circle of the new financial oligarchy. Contrary to most contemporary states Russia cannot refer to historical experiences of successful alliance policies. Russian identity has never been associated with integration and community, but, on the contrary, with supremacy over other states. Although the threat has receded under the present leadership, first warning signals indicate the possibility of an isolationist foreign policy as, several times in recent years, Russia has consciously ignored international norms: the threat of terminating the Treaty on Convential Forces in Europe (CFE); the war in Chechnya; but also the way it dealt with cultural treasures carried off during World War II ("trophy art"). If this tendency were to be reinforced under the influence of national-authoritarian forces, the "Cold Peace" between Russia and the West, conjured up by President Yeltsin, could soon become reality.

Russia in confrontation

The trend towards a diversification of Russia's external relations is gaining ground to the detriment of the country's western orientation.[77] Although Russia depends on the West in terms of its economy and financial policy, alienation from, and distance to, the West is growing. It is not only extremist circles which consider the extension of western influence as a security threat. With nationalist or even chauvinist forces gaining ever more influence, antagonism and confrontation could assert themselves, especially if the NATO debate came to a head.[78] The importance given by Russian foreign policy to relations with the West continuously decreases. "Euro-Atlantic" forces are systematically pushed back. Disappointment with lacking western support and the hardships of the reform course is accompanied by fears of being excluded from the new European security order. Russia's ambitions for geopolitical influence and parity were one of the main reasons for the East-West conflict after 1945. If escalating towards confrontation, super-power ambitions of the new Russia would again conjure up the danger of bipolarism in Europe, with unforeseeable consequences for European and global politics.

The West is neither interested in having to deal with an isolated Russia nor with a Russia bent on confrontation. If either of these scenarios came to a head, this would not only mean that the massive western economic and financial aid would have been wasted and western goodwill towards Russia exhausted. All sides would also be threatened by a new spiral of expensive armament. Peace and stability all over Europe would be threatened by a series of risks: the destabilisation of Central and Eastern Europe and the Balkans as well as jeopardising the long-term integration of both regions into Euro-Atlantic structures; an increasing nuclear danger if international efforts at disarmament and non-proliferation were questioned; the development of potential new conflicts at the future borders between an enlarged EU and NATO and Russia and the other western CIS neighbour republics.

---

77 Foye, Stephen: A Hardened Stance on Foreign Policy, in: Transition 9 June 1995, pp. 36ff.
78 On the hardening of Russian policy towards the west, already visible before the presidential elections, cf. Timmermann, Heinz: Rußlands Außenpolitik: Die europäische Dimension, in: Osteuropa No. 6, 1995, pp. 495ff.

Nuclear and ecological time bombs

With the end of the Cold War the nuclear era has not come to an end. On the contrary, the danger of a nuclear escalation is greater now than when both super-powers were confronting each other. Due to the risks of nuclear proliferation, the dangers of a "Cold Peace" turn into a crisis scenario. Europe in particular is in danger. An enlarged Europe moves into direct neighbourhood of the still virulent legacies of the Cold War.

The nuclear time bomb of the USSR is still ticking in four CIS countries – in Kazakhstan, Ukraine, Belarus and in Russia itself. Kazakhstan was the first successor republic to hand over all strategic arms to Russia and ratify the nuclear Non-Proliferation Treaty (NPT); it now feels particularly abandoned by the western community. The world's largest nuclear test area in Semipalatinsk has been closed since 1991. However, according to estimates, up to two million people have suffered from radioactive secondary injuries.[79] Moreover Kazakhstan represents another impending danger: in 1993/94 a cache with 600 kg highly enriched uranium (HEU) was found accidentally. In a secret operation the USA successfully managed to purchase the material from Kazakhstan and fly it out of the country before a third party could lay its hands on it.[80] Since then unknown secret stocks of fissile material have become an additional risk of the post-Soviet era.

The dangers of outmoded nuclear power plants in the CIS successor states remain an equally uncalculable danger. Belarus suffers more than any other state from the aftermath of the Chernobyl disaster. Up to now it has been impossible fully to estimate the extent of the long-term damage in Ukraine. Nevertheless the first "nuclear summit" of the G 7 in Moscow in 1996 showed that, even ten years after the catastrophe, the final shutdown of the reactor causing the accident is still in the dim distance.[81] Despite the announcement that the two reactor blocks still working were to be shut down until the year 2000, no binding document has been finalised. Meanwhile another 13 risk reactors of the RBMK-type

---

79 Bhavna, Dave: Kazahkstan Staggers Under Its Nuclear Burden, in: Transition 17 November 1995, pp. 12ff.
80 Cf. Potter, Willian C.: The "Sapphire" File: Lessons for International Non-proliferation Cooperation, ibd., p. 14ff.
81 Frankfurter Allgemeine Zeitung of 22 April 1996.

are still operating on the territory of the former Soviet Union: two in Lithuania and eleven in Russia. Considerable investment has been made into their security. However, the very interim financial aid of the West has contributed to keeping these risk reactors on the grid.[82] Repeated reports about accidents in Russian nuclear power plants indicate that further catastrophes caused by (military and civil) nuclear reactors from the Soviet era continue to remain possible.

Nowhere are the nuclear legacies bigger than in Russia.[83] Paradoxically, problems for Russia have become drastically more acute by the disarmament and denuclearisation of the neighbour states. The country is confronted with enormous security problems by the demolition programme of the START I Treaty alone. The transport, storage and disposal of nuclear material have become more uncertain than ever in today's Russia. Returning thousands of partly outmoded nuclear warheads from Kazakhstan, Ukraine and Belarus increases the technical risks considerably.[84] The ratification of the START II Treaty is still far from certain. However, even in case of its being implemented, the disposal of further thousands of nuclear warheads in Russia would initially heighten the nuclear risk. Further aspects of the Russian nuclear policy also cause concern:

- nuclear arms are still defined as instruments to guarantee super-power status and "to enforce geopolitical aims";
- the nuclear programmes of anti-western states, such as Iran, Cuba etc. are supported;
- continued efforts to obscure information about Russian nuclear stocks and plans (in 1995, supervision about military plants was withdrawn from the nuclear control authority);
- the public is insufficiently informed about the risks of the Russian nuclear programme while militant action is taken against environmental activists (thus, for example, a Russian staff member of the Norwegian environmental organisation Bellona was arrested).

---

82 Cf. Results of the Viennese Chernobyl Conference in April 1996, Süddeutsche Zeitung of 10 April 1996. On a critical analysis of western nuclear programmes in Eastern Europe cf. World Information Service on Energy (WISE): News Communique 449/450, 1996, pp. 4ff.
83 On a comprehensive analysis cf. Deutsches Institut für Wirtschaftsforschung (ed.): Nukleare Umweltgefährdung in Rußland, in: Wochenbericht No. 21, 1996, pp. 359–369.
84 Bukharin, Oleg: Meeting the Challenges of Dismantlement, Transition 17 November 1995, pp. 30ff.

Trafficking in uncontrolled nuclear material from the former Soviet Union, from Russia in particular, is a new danger. According to an American study, the highest security risk for the West today lies in a nuclear disaster caused by "nuclear anarchy". The study proves that 100 000 nuclear weapons and units of fissile material are still stored on the territory of the former USSR, scattered among approximately 300 different plants. Insufficient surveillance and security systems, an outmoded infrastructure, poverty and corruption have increased possibilities of stealing and trafficking in nuclear material ("loose nukes"). To date only six cases have been clearly documented; the estimated number of unknown cases, however, remains alarmingly high and threatens to increase.[85]

For all the dramatically high nuclear risks, the other ecological legacies from the former USSR must not be forgotten. All CIS republics have taken over an overwhelming number of environmental burdens from Soviet times.[86] The difficult transformation years have not brought any visible improvement in environmental protection. On the contrary, due to the increasing erosion of equipment and plants, chronical security deficits have further intensified. Although production is constantly falling, the number of serious accidents in Russia is rising.[87] The ecological crisis and increasing risks of accidents have additional negative effects on the economic and social crisis in most CIS states and the health condition of their populations. All over the CIS region, with especially high concentration in Russia and Central Asia, growing air and water pollution, ground erosion, damage done to the forests and desertification may have socially explosive consequences (costs for public health, migration), which could threaten the economic development of the whole post-Soviet space.

---

85 Allison, Graham T. et al.: Avoiding Nuclear Anarchy – Containing the Threat of Loose Russian Nuclear Weapons and Fissile Material, Cambridge (Mass.) 1996.
86 S. Golitsyn, Georgii C.: Ecological Problems in the CIS during the Transitional Period, in: Transition 8 January 1993, pp. 33 ff.
87 For a comprehensive analysis of non-nuclear security deficits in Russia cf. Weißenburger, Ulrich: Sicherheitsmängel und Störfallrisiken als Problem der russischen Wirtschafts- und Umweltpolitik, Teil 1: Umweltgefährdung durch Sicherheitsdefizite im nichtnuklearen Bereich, in: Berichte des BIOst No. 14, 1996.

III. Aims of the EU *Ostpolitik*

In order to be able to ensure peace and stability all over Europe, the framework for supporting the three regions must be distinctly defined in future. For that purpose it is necessary critically to take stock of western aid to date.

1. Central and Eastern Europe: integration into the EU

The European Union has, by offering the option for joining in the Association Agreements, committed itself to an eastern enlargement. The approximation and integration of the Central and Eastern European states into the EU aim at consolidating the transformation processes and ascertaining stability and prosperity in Europe. The all-European economic and political future depends on the success of this historic project. The EU enlargement follows the perspective "to realise an increasingly closer union of the peoples of Europe", which was laid down in the Maastricht Treaty. At the same time it provides a great chance to outline a political space based on the principles of political democracy as well as further to explore new, expanding markets: on the one hand the original number of EU members will more than quadruple by the enlargement; the Union as alliance of western-style democracies will be strengthened considerably. On the other hand, with another 106 million consumers – approximately 30 percent of the present EU's population – the European internal market will develop new dynamic force in terms of growth. Labour costs, which are considerably lower in the Central and Eastern European countries, offer interesting prospects for an effective allocation of the European factor. The EU's disadvantages compared with Japan and the USA could be overcome, and its international competitiveness could be much improved.

Although the CEE states have a firm perspective of integration, the question of when, and how, which states will be able to join the EU – and what the Union's future structures will look like – is still open. At the Maastricht summit in December 1995 the association states were merely promised that six months after the end of the IGC negotiations on their accession were to be entered into, which would be based on opinions of the European Commission about each country. However, the further course of the EU's structural reform largely continues to be an unclear issue. In consequence, the future accession strategy and the timetable for a first integration round are equally unclear. Therefore the EU ought to devise a coherent integration strategy for the transition period until negotiations are started in order to give the CEE states political, economic and psychological security for their planning. A definite schedule is of essential importance to the association states. Firstly, it would, despite all hardships, contribute to maintaining the necessary dynamic force in transformation and reform processes. Secondly, the widely-accepted consensus in the CEE states on a further orientation towards the West could be maintained. Clearly defined integration prospects would not least be a basic precondition for another injection of capital in Central and Eastern Europe by foreign enterprises.

In the course of the eastern enlargement, considerable adjustments are required from the Union, but also from the Central and Eastern European states. In the coming transition period, existing structures of cooperation between the EU and the association states should be developed further; the different lines of reform ought to be coordinated timewise. The pre-accession strategy adopted at the Essen summit (December 1994) and the Commission's "White Paper" on the preparation of the associated states for integration into the internal market form constituent prerequisites.[88] Within the framework of the "structured dialogue" on the ministerial level, the CEE states have already been integrated into fields of common interest and trans-European dimensions (energy, environment, traffic, science etc.), the Common Foreign and Security Policy (CFSP) and the fields of legal and home affairs. However, in the future, cooperation must be organised in a much more substantial and efficient way. Moreover further methods are to be developed in order to give the CEE states a share in concrete measures of the EU (declarations, *demarches*).

The Association Agreements form an important framework for the political, economic and financial integration of the Central and Eastern European states into the EU. However, up to now the agreements have partly missed their target on the economic level. It is still the EU which profits to a much higher degree from trade with the Central and Eastern European countries. Since 1993 the EU has registered high export surpluses, mainly in agricultural trade, because the agricultural sector has, to a considerable extent, been excluded from trade liberalisation. In addition the EU has made imports in the iron and steel sector more difficult by introducing anti-dumping measures (art. 30 of the Association Agreements) so that the Central and Eastern European states have until now been unable to make use of their comparative competitive advantages; in consequence their balance-of-payments crisis has further increased. The EU's aim should be, however, further to accelerate the progress of trade liberalisation in order to integrate the CEE countries better into the world trade.

The development of the infrastructure and the intraregional cooperation in Central and Eastern Europe are supported by the PHARE programme. By the end of 1995, the EU had made ECU 5.5 bn in non-repayable subsidies available. By the end of the year 2000, the annual allocation is to be increased from ECU 1.1 bn to ECU 1.6 bn. In addition the Commission is planing measures to make the technical realisation of the PHARE programme more efficient. The programme is to be further decentralised. The Central and Eastern European countries' implementation capacities are to be improved. A big share of the funds destined for administrative purposes is still spent in the EU states, which has proved

---

88 Cf. European Commission: White Paper on the Preparation of the associated Countries of Central and Eastern Europe for integration into the internal market of the Union, COM (95) 163 final, Brussels 1995.

to be a problem. This is all the more alarming since – measured against Central and Eastern Europe's external financial needs – the PHARE funds on the whole are too small (approximately 5 percent of the annual subsidies available from the EU's structural fund).

2. The Balkans: stabilising peace

As a motor and framework of European unification, the European Union will only remain credible if it succeeds in starting a stable and peaceful development in the Balkans. An efficient Balkan policy of the EU will turn the scales in favour of a permanent stabilisation of the region. Moreover the risks of war, potential ethnic conflicts, pauperisation, waves of migration and political chaos do not only threaten peace in the region, but also the EU member countries. Thus more is at stake in the Balkans for the EU than for individual states or any other international organisation.

As far as the aim of stabilising the region is concerned, EU policy to date has to be critically analysed. A common policy towards the states of the former Yugoslavia has failed not so much because of different interests of the individual member states, but rather because the Common Foreign and Security Policy lacked coordination, conceptional design and realisation.[89] Interests between the western countries are certainly not as different as foreign-policy reports suggest. The importance of geopolitical orientation, traditional historical loyalties and religious-cultural sympathies is overestimated. On the contrary, the problem is that the EU has not managed to transform its member states' common values and objectives into consistent political positions and strategies.

The inconsistent policy of the EU towards Yugoslavia contributed to the escalation of the conflicts and accepted countless victims as well as expulsion and destruction. The EU member states recognised the republics of the federation, Slovenia, Croatia and Bosnia-Herzegovina, as in-

---

[89] Calic, Marie-Janine: Der Krieg in Bosnien-Herzegowina. Ursachen, Konfliktstrukturen, internationale Lösungsversuche, Frankfurt 1995; Gnesotto, Nicole: Lessons of Yugoslavia, WEU Institute for Security Studies, Chaillot Papers March 1994.

dependent states but did not face up to the consequences and protect their territorial integrity against Serb aggressors. At the same time, they prevented Bosnia-Herzegovina from obtaining the necessary means to defend itself effectively against the attacks by supporting a UN arms embargo, which aggravated the inferiority of the Bosnian side. This misguided decision was particularly fatal since the international community did not guarantee the security of the Bosnian population and intervened much too late.[90]

The policy of recognition pursued towards the Yugoslav republics has had serious consequences. It has furthermore shown that the EU member states do not sufficiently coordinate their policies, neither among each other, nor in their dealings with the EU presidency. Even though foreign-policy decision-makers in the EU and the member states have learnt from their experience of 1991/2, there are still problems of synchronising activities. Thus there is a lack of coordination between individual political spheres, in particular between foreign and security policy and single steps of economic cooperation and integration. The Balkan policy of the EU and the USA has been characterised in recent years by different assessments of military armament which have made crisis management more difficult; to date, they have not yet been adjusted.

There is a basic conflict between political approaches which make aid programmes and stages of cooperation dependent on advance concessions and compliance and approaches which understand aid and cooperation as steps towards a change of behaviour. As yet, EU policy has not been able to clarify the relation between "conditional" and "functional" political approaches sufficiently. The existing institutional network between the EU, the Council of Europe and the OSCE with their different decision-making mechanisms, interests and political traditions does not allow Europe to employ its moral, political and diplomatic authority in a coherent and consistant way. As a result of these coordination problems, the EU's political behaviour creates uncertainty in the region, appears incalculable and constantly offers the opportunity to play off individual member states and EU institutions against each other.

---

90 Rieff, David: Slaughterhouse. Bosnia and the Failure of the West, New York 1995; Zumach, Andreas: Weltpolitische Agonie. Großmächte zwischen Ohnmacht und Kollaboration, in: Lettre International No. 31, 1995, pp. 104–105.

Until now the goals the EU set itself in its Balkan policy have proved to be too ambitious in principle, as the EU could not devise feasible ways and means to implement them. Ambitious political forms of organisation, such as the Bosnian-Herzegovin state structure, are precarious because they are not based on a far-reaching institutional change, or because this change – in case it is intended – does not take place within the same period of time or can only be planned timewise to a limited degree. Bosnia-Herzegovina is threatened with collapse as the political actors still orientate themselves on the conflict patterns of war. Introducing ambitious objectives – as, for example, multi-ethnicity or a federal system – against the opposition of nationalist élites and the population groups mobilised by them seems to be a futile attempt. The EU's efforts to direct the peace process are concentrated too much on the level of governments and political leaderships; cooperation between economic actors and social initiatives are, by contrast, insufficiently taken into account.

A stable development of the Balkan region must start from the present borders. Given the fragile political order and the history of drawing arbitrary borders, a change of the territorial status quo would give new impulses, whose consequences could not be disregarded. At the same time those in power within existing states must not be allowed to violate human and civil rights and to exert violence against minorities and dissidents. Economic aid and all models of cooperation should therefore be bound to plausible, checkable and predictable preconditions. The EU ought to give all countries of the region a clear perspective for integration, which would in the long term lead from trade and cooperation agreements via association agreements to full EU membership. As the political and economic élites of the Balkan countries are highly interested in integrating into the European internal market, the EU can use cooperation, association and integration as a means to promote democracy, market economy and constitutional systems.

In order to increase the coherence and the predictability of its Balkan policy, the EU must improve coordination among its member states. By reforming the decision-making mechanism in the Common Foreign and Security Policy, all member states would be induced to develop common interests and to harmonise their Balkan policies more efficiently. It is furthermore necessary to improve coordination on several inter-organisational levels: between the EU and the most important international organisations (OSCE, NATO and UN); between the EU, the USA and Russia; and finally between the EU and its member states and the associated states in the region, i. e. Greece, Bulgaria, Romania, Slovenia and Hungary.

The EU must direct its *Ostpolitik* in the region towards establishing various structures of dialogue aimed at the peaceful settlement of conflicts and at cooperation, and towards convincing actors to participate. Within this framework actors should be given the opportunity of defining the modalities of their future coexistence and of institutionalising concepts for political order. Multilateral and bilateral dialogue as well as dialogue on the level of governments and societal actors, between states and within the individual states should be initiated and supported.

The numerous existing levels of European integration could be used in order to bring about a modernisation of the Balkan countries. The numerous experiences from cooperation within the integration space EU in particular offer a valuable repertory of tools to strengthen civil society and develop economic and political structures in individual countries. By supporting independent organisations and actors, the political and economic transformation initiated by the governing élites will gain ground. At the same time alternatives for ethnic mobilisation will be promoted. An extensive process of socio-economic modernisation, sped up by economic development, is the only means to overcome ethnic differences and the weak civil society permanently.

3. Russia and the CIS: cooperation and "strategic partnership"

Stabilising the post-Soviet space is another key to stability and peace in the whole of Europe. From this perspective it is one of the greatest challenges to a new European *Ostpolitik* to develop a strategy for partnership and cooperation with Russia and the future European CIS neighbour states Belarus and Ukraine (in the long term Moldavia, too).

Six years after the collapse of the Soviet Union a critical stock-taking

of the present policy towards Russia and the CIS must take place. Whereas in the post-war-period a unique dynamism led to the creation of numerous international institutions, the West has reacted in a passive and conceptionally inflexible way to the break-up of the Soviet Union:
- Western policy towards Russia and the CIS continues to fall behind the process of opening Euro-Atlantic structures for the Central and Eastern European states. From the very beginning the integration of Central and Eastern Europe should have been complemented by co-operation and partnership with Russia and the leading CIS states. Until now the West has failed to develop a coherent overall concept. A policy of "Russia first" has too long been adhered to. While in the case of Ukraine the West was very late in developing a parallel strategy to support national independence, it has not even started thinking about it in the case of Belarus and Moldavia.
- The transfer of western resources is still too insignificant to promote the transformation process in the CIS states effectively. OECD reports prove that the extent of western aid and support measures for the CIS countries is alarmingly low: whereas western aid for Estonia made up just under US$ 50 (1993) per inhabitant, the average per-capita amount in the CIS states has up to now been considerably under US$ 10.[91] In addition, in the case of Russia the political possibilities of aid programmes to give the West a chance to exert its influence have been overestimated. In Central and Eastern Europe the EU's integration strategy comprises concrete directive possibilities, but the external influence on Russia's development is increasingly limited.
- NATO's confused and ill-considered course in the enlargement question has contributed to estranging Russia and the West. NATO submitted its "political framework declaration" and the foundations of a future policy of "dialogue and cooperation" too late (September 1995) and even then they were only made known insufficiently. Furthermore a restricted eastern enlargement of NATO threatens to intensify confusion unless it is accompanied by a well-designed concept for the other CEE states; a security partnership with Russia and the European

---

91 Cf. OECD: Aid and other Resource Flows to the Central and Eastern European Countries and the New Independent States of the Former Soviet Union in 1992 and 1993, Paris 1995.

CIS states must, in particular, be confirmed by a treaty binding both sides. In the future it is necessary to build up a realistic political framework for the cooperation with Russia and the CIS states. Within these limits, the forms of cooperation must be evaluated much more purposefully. Beyond the narrow horizon of NATO enlargement, a balance of common security threats and interests, based on a code of common principles, must be made the starting point of future neighbourly relations.

- On principle, rather than creating new institutions, existing structures are to be further developed and interwoven into a new institutional network. Apart from NATO the EU will have a key role. The EU is Russia's direct neighbour, most important trading partner and main actor in the strategy of supporting the country, and to an increasing extent the other CIS neighbour states, too.[92] Therefore it must develop a long-term concept for the CIS. Since Finland became a member of the EU in 1995, the EU and Russia have shared a long common border. The eastern enlargement will raise the question of adequate relations with the future neighbour states Belarus and Ukraine. In consequence the "Action Plan for Russia"[93] (adopted in May 1996) and that for Ukraine (adopted in December 1996) should be complemented by an action plan for Belarus, and in the long term for Moldavia.
- The EU must take two further aspects into consideration: whereas in Central and Eastern Europe the EU remains the leading actor, the European policy towards Russia and the CIS should be integrated into a trilateral "strategic partnership" with the United States. It is equally important to start including those Central and Eastern European association countries which will soon form the eastern borders of the EU. The future EU member states must, already in the course of their association process, complement their western integration by an active *Ostpolitik*.
- The policy towards Russia remains the most important challenge to the future European *Ostpolitik*. There can only be stability and peace

---

[92] For an overview of EU policy towards Russia cf. Timmermann, Heinz: Die Europäische Union und Rußland – Dimensionen und Perspektiven der Partnerschaft, in: Integration, No. 4 1996, pp. 195–207.
[93] Cf. Agence Europe of 16 May 1996.

in Europe in cooperation with, but not against, Russia. Major aims are the extensive deepening and institutionalisation of relations between Russia and the leading actors EU and NATO. New forms of treaties and contracts must be created for that purpose. Initially it will be decisive that Russia itself understands its own national interest in a stable partnership with the West. At the same time the West must be interested in the stable development of the national independence of Belarus and Ukraine and, in the long term, of the other CIS states as well. It should equally be in the interest of the West that individual republics are integrated step by step, based on the principle of free-will decisions. A differentiated overall concept for a western CIS policy is required. A policy of "direct neighbourhood" must be complemented by cooperation and partnership with the other CIS states. New chances resulting from geographical vicinity must be checked out and developed on the basis of common interests.

– Democracy and market economy remain the preconditions of a stable neighbourhood with Russia, Belarus and Ukraine. Only democratic and liberal-minded states make reliable and cooperative neighbours. The long-term democratic development of the three western successor states of the USSR continue to be in the West's own interest. The West must clearly stress that it wants its future neighbours to be efficient economic partners. A modern Russia, integrated into the world economy, will be the nearest and most important trading and cooperation partner of the future Europe.

– Finally, Europe must not leave it to the USA to solve problems of nuclear security. This includes the secondary risks of military and civil use of nuclear power, notably the risk of uncontrolled proliferation. The danger of "loose nukes" is not taken seriously enough by the USA either. In the EU, however, the public has not even realised that this issue exists.

IV. Strategies of a new *Ostpolitik*

The different aims which European policy pursues in Central and Eastern Europe, the Balkans and Russia and the CIS are to be implemented by working out specific strategic approaches for the three regions. What is in particular to be envisaged is a strategy for enlargement for Central and Eastern Europe, a strategy for peace for the Balkans and a strategy for cooperation and partnership with Russia and the CIS. All three approaches must be complemented by a concept for overall European neighbourhood, which can guarantee the integration of different areas.

1. Central and Eastern Europe: strategy for enlargement

The EU, NATO and the Western European Union (WEU) are faced with an historical task. The different programmes of eastern enlargement aim at securing political and social stability and prosperity all over Europe. When integrating the new Central and Eastern European democracies, the organisations must remain capable to act and work. The EU is required to make particularly strong efforts in order not to make the next enlargement round founder on the Union's structural deficits. Therefore the reforms of the Central and Eastern European states and the EU's structural reform must be sped up simultaneously. Both reform pro-

cesses are interdependent. The successful eastern enlargement of the EU will depend on the nexus between the following components:
- the Central and Eastern European states' readiness further to adjust to the EU;
- the Union's political willingness to create the preconditions for an eastern enlargement by internal reforms and balancing interests;
- the structuring of the integration process into scheduled stages and definitely fixed association groups;
- the EU's further development within the framework of differentiated integration.

Efforts to be made by the associated states

Now, as before, the CEE states themselves will have to carry the main burden of economic and political reforms. They must continue to prepare themselves for EU membership and create the preconditions in order to accept the valid acquis communautaire of the Union. In many problem areas, the only way for the EU's active involvement is to support the states.

The "White Paper" on the preparation for the internal market offers the Central and Eastern European states a guideline for legal approximation, technical harmonisation and the introduction of European standards. The extensive work in the field of legal approximation must be done by the associated countries themselves, but the EU should make the necessary know-how available. Major importance is to be given to working out and implementing national strategies which serve to shape the countries' own priorities and schedules for adjusting legal regulations. Here the associated states would be best advised to intensify cooperation with the EU, in particular with the information office established in 1996 for just this purpose. Moreover targeted measures for the in-service training of civil servants in administration and justice in the CEE states are required so that the new legal regulations can be applied.

In order to improve competition in Central and Eastern Europe, national authorities must ensure that the competition law is consistently developed further. All subsidies will have to be strictly controlled since, in case of EU membership, many current payments in the integration states would be considered government aid. In every country a national authority should be commissioned to examine all state subsidies. Within the financial sector exchange rates must be given a chance to develop properly. More stable exchange rates could attract more international capital and also direct it into those sectors which due to lacking markets have hardly seemed attractive. The privatisation of banks must be accelerated in all association states.

In order to consolidate the reforms, investment promotion in the private and the state sector is particularly important. The focus should be placed on strengthening export-oriented small and medium-sized enterprises and improving infrastructure and environmental protection. Here the state and the banks will have to stimulate investment by creating more favourable framework conditions. In view of the high costs of finance, ivestors show little inclination to invest in the domestic market. Therefore a reduction of lending rates ought to be given first priority. Depending on the respective countries, this reduction can be harmonised with the fight against inflation. By improving legislation and opening markets the state itself can encourage foreign investors to commit themselves more deeply.

With a view to EU integration, a major part must also be played by intraregional cooperation in Central and Eastern Europe. Firstly, regional integration capacity is increasingly becoming a criterion by which the associated states' integration capacity is measured. Secondly, regional cooperation can contribute to defusing problems in international relations and stabilising the region of Central and Eastern Europe as a whole. Intensified cooperation should mainly take place by further developing CEFTA. Romania and Bulgaria, but also the Baltic states, ought to be accepted as members as soon as they fulfil order and trade policy prerequisites. If, furthermore, free-trade principles were made to include all industrial and agricultural products, this would contribute to intensifying competition among the CEFTA states.

Given the rapidly growing poverty in Central and Eastern Europe, ensuring a minimum of social stability is becoming more and more urgent. Solidarity and mutual responsibility in society and the reinforcement of personal responsibility must, under the pressure of tight money, be balanced anew. In the new democracies social security and peace will be founded on the establishment of minimal social standards. The new phenomenon of unemployment represents one of the most difficult problems of the Eastern European transformation societies. In the labour market policy priority should be given to job-creation schemes (e. g. by training programmes). The pension systems, which are financed by adjustable contributions, must be further developed in such a way that private pension schemes can become the second pillar of the pension system. This will help to overcome current funding problems and secure the pensions of succeeding generations. Great structural changes are also required in the public health sector. Health protection, safety at work and an improved system of handling statistical data are important future tasks to guarantee that programmes of social support are directed straight at the target.

In addition, environmental policy in the Central and Eastern European countries must be given higher priority. In future economic and ecological modernisation should be more closely connected. EU integration will certainly be accelerated if further adjustment to the environmental standards of the EU in the fields of air and water pollution, nature conservation and waste disposal is achieved, and standards are nationally implemented. More intensively than before, a well-aimed strategy of information must be employed to sensitise populations and companies for environmental issues. Many problems require transnational solutions. Therefore closer cooperation with the EU (via bilateral or regional projects) and the European Environmental Agency ought to be strived for.

Organised crime and the fight against it must also become a focus of attention in future. Up to now legislation in Central and Eastern Europe has not yet found any adequate instruments to meet the growing menace of criminal structures. Improved regulations are required so as to reinforce the effectiveness of investigative authorities and jurisdiction. At the same time specialist staff of law courts and police authorities need qualified training. The financial markets also require new legal regulations. Money laundering, mainly in the banking system, must be stopped. Future cooperation with Europol (European Police Authority) is of great importance in order to better coordinate investigation activities on the international level. Europol ought to be specially authorized to investigate on its own in the fight against crime; the number of departments (apart from the anti-drug squad in The Hague) should be increased.

Whether, and to which extent, EU integration is accepted by the population remains of basic importance. However, in all Central and Eastern European states knowledge about the EU, its institutions and decision-making mechanisms and costs and benefits of full membership is poor. More initiatives within the field of education and communication are required to fight against this information deficit. Educational institutions, political parties and the media should initiate national debates on Europe in all CEE states. For the purpose of information and consultation, governments could open Euro-centres or Europe Houses in different parts of their countries. The educational authorities are also called for: new professions and educational and training programmes must be established. Educational programmes relating to European issues are to be developed, in particular for the political élites. In addition, school twinning, exchange programmes for professors and students as well as programmes promoting foreign-language education ought to be further intensified in cooperation with the EU.

Internal reforms of the EU and balance of interests

Managing the EU integration of the Central and Eastern European states will be much more complicated than the southern enlargements of 1981 and 1986. Firstly, after having fully established the internal market, the EU is today characterised by a denser level of harmonisation and regulation. Each new candidate for accession has to accept these common assets. Secondly, the financial situation of the EU member states has worsened. The acceptance of new, structurally weak member states inevitably creates additional burdens; the readiness and capacity to bear them has decreased. Finally, the large number of countries which want to join the EU will be too much for the political structures as well as the available resources of the EU if the existing regulations are simply adhered to without any modification. A Union enlarged to such an extent will only function under considerably modified conditions. These will have to be carefully prepared in the run-up to an enlargement.

Therefore the eastern enlargement increases the need to reform the EU institutions: capacity for action must be made more effective and decision-making processes will have to be simplified. At the same time agricultural and structural policy are to be reorganised in order to guarantee that a larger and more heterogeneous Union can permanently be financed. These reforms will be the prerequisites if an "EU of 27" is to be politically and economically efficient. Therefore their implementation will have an important place on the European agenda in the years to come. The reform of the decision-making processes is to be clarified until 1997 within the framework of the Intergovernmental Conference on the revision of the Maastricht Treaty. The funding guidelines laid down in the Delors II package will be discontinued in 1999. When the EU's financial equipment is developed further, the consequences of the eastern enlargement will have to be taken into account.

In order to make speedy decision-making processes in an enlarged EU possible, multiple-vote decisions in the Council of Ministers will have to be increased.[94] At present the unanimity rule, which allows each member state to obstruct decisions, is valid in many fields of common policies (e. g. taxes, structural funds, Common Foreign and Security Policy). Furthermore, the weighting of votes in the Council of Ministers should be altered so that, upon enlargement, it will become impossible for the smaller member states to outvote the big states. In order to strenghten external and internal continuity, an elected Union presidency ought to be preferred to the strict rotation system of the presidency in the Council of Ministers. According to this procedure, the member states would elect one of their members for president, whose term would last at least one year. At the same time this act of voting would increase the Council's legitimacy and improve its cohesion.

The Commission's ability to work in an enlarged Union could be improved by reorganising the Commission according to the number of portfolios required and not on the basis of national quotas. The president of the Commission would distribute portfolios within the Commission. By establishing the number of commissioners required according to du-

---

94 Cf. on the proposals of the institutional reforms: Weidenfeld, Werner (ed.): Reform der Europäischen Union. Materialien zur Revision des Maastrichter Vertrages 1996, Gütersloh 1995.

ties the Commission could, at the same time, be reduced in size. To guarantee the smooth functioning of the European Parliament, the number of seats should be limited to well under 700. The different national voting systems should also be replaced by a uniform European electoral law. National quotas in proportion to the population of the member state would be best, so as to strengthen the legitimacy of the European Parliament. In order to improve democratic control, the rights of the European Parliament to participate in decisions are to be developed further. Within its responsibilities, EU legislation should in principle be the result of common and equal decision by the European Parliament and the Council of Ministers. The present system of participation in decision-making processes is to be simplified and made the regular system within the framework of a two-chamber system.

Reforming the Common Agricultural Policy will be indispensable if European agricultural production is to be controlled in a more efficient way and the CEE states are to join the EU. At present agricultural products in the association states are only subsidised at 20 percent, compared with an EU average of almost 50 percent. In order to cut EU subsidies further, the agricultural reform of the EU, started in 1992, must be continued in a more decisive way than to date. In concrete terms this means that the gradual cut in support prices will also have to be applied to vegetable agricultural products (fruit, vegetables and wine), which have until now not been included, and animal products (pork, eggs and poultry); they make up more than half of the agricultural production of the EU. Grain prices must be reduced further to the level of world market prices. This is in line with the agreements negotiated in the Uruguay round of GATT, which provide for a stronger market orientation of agricultural policy. In order to compensate for income losses, EU farmers should receive per-equation payments. In addition, the reduction of present price supports in favour of direct income supports should be linked with ecological requirements by binding payments to corresponding services supplied by the farmers (environmental protection, nature conservation).

Moreover, reorganising structural policy is indispensable in order to guarantee that it can be financed, and remains efficient, in the long term. The integration of the Central and Eastern European states will considerably change the prosperity gap in the EU. The population and the surface area of the EU will enlarge by a third; at the same time the average per-capita GDP in the associated countries makes up less than a quarter of the EU average. Since all CEE states will continue to fulfil the presently valid criteria for receiving support from the EU structural funds for several years, the funds will have to be massively increased. Readiness to pay considerably higher contributions hardly exists so that the reform of the regional policy must aim at concentrating activities geographically and thematically. In order to guarantee that funds are efficiently applied, the recipient states' capacity for absorbing them – approximately 3 – 5 percent of the GDP, according to previous experience – ought to be made a criterion for allocation. The present criteria for allocating the structural funds also encourage carelessness as funds need not be repaid. Part of the monies from the structural funds should therefore be allocated as (free-of-rate) loans. Finally, all approved projects must be better monitored and evaluated by the Commission.

The eastern enlargement forces the present EU members to clarify their objectives and interests as regards European policy. Therefore the eastern enlargement is not least a question of balancing interests. Each new enlargement requires that all present members can rest assured that their interests are adequately taken into account in an "EU of 27". Here mainly the southern EU states are concerned. Therefore, before an eastern enlargement takes place, it is to be guaranteed that one focus of the structural and cohesion policy will – also in the future – be on the Mediterranean region. In order to ease the financial burdens for the present EU members, the CEE states' integration into problematic fields – such as agricultural and structural policy – could take place gradually. This is to be guaranteed by the well-considered determination of interim periods and the application of protective clauses.

Structuring the integration process

According to the decision of the Madrid summit, integration negotiations with the Central and Eastern European states are to be entered into six months after the end of the IGC, i. e. presumably in 1998. At that time the Commission should give a concrete date for the integration of a first group of accession candidates. In the EU, and in those states which want to join it, this would ensure the pressure required in order to realise this political aim. Under the precondition of special interim periods for the joining countries, the earliest possible date for accession would be the year 2000. Until then the institutional reform of the EU must be finished and financial planning must be reorganised so that the Union will have completed a first basic reform stage.

Until then the Union must clarify the way in which the pending integration negotiations will take place in principle. Negotiations should simultaneously be entered into with all CEE states ("starting-line model") instead of beginning with a special group of candidates ("group model"). If the principle of equality is maintained when talks about integration are started, this will guarantee that the Union keeps the necessary flexibility for the gradual enlargement process. A simultaneous start of negotiations would, above all, prevent those CEE states which would not be represented in a first enlargement round from letting up. Diverging tendencies in the region would be unnecessarily reinforced if some candidates were "eliminated" by group or individual talks.

If negotiations were simultaneously started, the EU would – based on individual country reports and clearly determined criteria for accession – not have to decide before 1999 which states were to be accepted in a first enlargement round. Before this could happen, the criteria which were laid down in 1993 by the European Council in Copenhagen would have to be made more concrete. A stable democracy; the capacity for accepting the acquis communautaire; a working market economy; and the willingness to join political as well as economic and monetary union were mentioned in Copenhagen. These criteria, however, remain vague and can hardly be quantified. Therefore it would be highly useful to specify them so as to make it easier for the Commission to evaluate the state of the integration capacity; the Central and Eastern European states would receive a new reform impetus and could head for the EU in a more determined way. The criterion of "establishing free-enterprise structures" must, in particular, be complemented by the determination of precise quantitative economic indicators (e. g. inflation rate, unemployment, foreign debt) and microeconomic criteria (e. g. privatisation, corporate debt, export structure of enterprises). At the same time additional criteria for the integration capacity must be considered. The focus should be on the CEE states' readiness for regional cooperation and their willingness to transfer sovereignty as well as on an active *Ostpolitik*.

The eastern enlargement of the EU will definitely come about in several stages. According to the presently valid criteria, the prospects of being represented in a first enlargement round are best for the Czech Republic, Poland, Hungary and Slovenia. In addition, Cyprus and Malta have already been promised to be accepted in a first round. More delicate is the question of the EU membership of the Baltic states. As they would not be represented in a first NATO enlargement, the problem of the Baltic states' security is more urgent. However, provided it fulfils the relevant criteria, one Baltic state should at least be represented in the first EU enlargement round. Given the progress made in the transformation process, Estonia has the best chances at present. With Slovenia in the south and Estonia in the north, apart from the core states in Central and Eastern Europe, the enlarged Union would thus include a Balkan state and a successor state of the Soviet Union respectively. At present, the integration of Slovakia, which due to its internal development threatens to drop out of the EU approximation process, remains a special problem. In terms of security policy, an early integration into the EU would also be important for Slovakia since it does not have any concrete prospects for joining NATO either. It is up to the Slovak government to use the historic chance of "returning to Europe" and try to fulfil the other criteria for EU membership.

Those Central and Eastern European states which would only be eligible for integration in a second round need particular support from the EU. They must be certain that they will not be discriminated against, but will still be directed consistently towards the EU. Therefore the proposal made by the French Foreign Minister de Charette ought to be reconsidered, who suggested that a"European conference" should be established after the IGC in order to further develop the strategy for approximation to, and integration into, the EU. All 15 member states and the 12 associated candidates for accession (Malta and Cyprus included) would be represented in such a conference. In case of first decisions on integration such a conference would offer the "candidates of the second round" an institutionalised forum to continue the approximation process.

Besides, new forms of political participation beyond the structured dialogue must be developed, in particular for the CEE states of the second round. Thus, they could already familiarise themselves with EU structures in the run-up to their integration. Simultaneously, societies should gradually be interlinked further, even in previously neglected fields (sciences, environment etc.). Finally it is necessary to improve market access for the associated states which remain outside the EU. A schedule for the elimination of tariffs and customs quota for industrial goods, textiles and agricultural products has been laid down in the Europe Agreements with Bulgaria, Romania, Slovenia and the Baltic states. It must be harmonised with the agreements made with the "Visegrád" states. In addition, the EU should inform the association states before it initiates anti-dumping or protective measures. If any dumping or damage could be proved, guaranteed minimum prices should clearly be given priority over tariffs. Finally the regulations of origin presently valid in trade must be changed: the EU should continue to work towards a full cumulation of origin in the trade with the associated states. Thus goods produced in Central and Eastern Europe would benefit from a preferential market access sooner.

Further development of the EU within the framework of differentiated integration

Apart from institutional reforms, policy adjustment and an enlargement concept, a European Union with 27 or more member states will also need a new strategy for integration which will take this new framework into consideration. The EU lacks a new blueprint in order to define its self-image, its future role and structure upon enlargement. The scenario of this large Europe makes it easy to detect that straight enlargement would result in the European Union's political, institutional and financial collapse. With the prospect of a European Union reaching from Sicily to the North Cape, and from the Atlantic to the river Bug, the European Union will come to the limits of the familiar, homogeneous system of integration, in which the process of European unification has steadily moved towards more integration on the supranational level. If progress is to be made in integration, it will be increasingly necessary to merge international and supranational integration. The spectrum of economic productivity and the variety of political interests will in the future be too wide so that it will be impossible strictly to follow the course traced out by the founder generations.

On principle it would certainly be possible to deal with the challenges of enlargement by taking decided steps towards more integration and full realisation of the supranational perspective, laid down in the agreements. Contrary to the previous enlargements of the European Community, future progress made in integration cannot only be guaranteed by managing the stages, i.e. by a directed succession of deepening and enlargement steps. Realising this scenario will also mean that for the next two decades the European Union will be in a phase of permanent change, adaptation and reorientation; its dimension will considerably exceed the patterns of enlargement and adjustment experienced in the course of the northern and southern enlargements in the 1970s and 1980s. Almost inevitably, "floating" towards the EU will result in a variable political geometry, following the dictates of the peculiarities of the countries willing to join the EU as well as the schedules which have been designed for the acceptance and application of the acquis communautaire of the European Union. The key question when it comes to deciding on whether this perspective can be realised, and is desirable, is how to ensure that the integration process remains stable, efficient and calculable during this procedure. A concept of differentiated integration is required, which enables the Union further to develop and, simultaneously, to enlarge.

The strategy of differentiated integration can be founded on the expertise of graduated integration and multiple speeds, i.e. for one part of the Union's member states, exceptions from the rule that Union law is to be fully applied can be made. These exceptions would be jointly agreed upon and they would usually be limited in terms of time. These procedures have been used successfully during previous enlargements. Exceptions are also found in the agreements, for example in the field of environmental protection and health care. Such measures, which are basically interim regulations, do not guarantee sufficient flexibility. If the integration is to be permanently differentiated in its intensity and the member states' roles and contributions are to be differentiated, the presently existing spectrum of graduated integration is no longer sufficient.

The alternative to concepts which depended on former circumstances lies in consciously differentiating integration, based on the status reached with the Maastricht Treaty.[95] Similar to the approach of graduated integration, developed in the 1970s, differentiated integration aims at advancing the development of the Union. In contrast to graduated integration, it does not require a homogeneous contractual framework and a binding time frame. Similar to the model of concentric circles[96], which was discussed at the end of the 1980s, differentiated integration is based on the formation of a nucleus. However, it is not restricted to one nucleus deepening all fields of integration at the same time, but tolerates several nuclei with different membership status. Given the fact that interests and performances within a Union of 27 or more states are different, differentiated integration supports the "opting in" of member states willing to work and produce – though not ad hoc and without obeying the rules. On the contrary, the basic principle of differentiation is to create structures organised in accordance with the specific demands of deepened integration and to gain the maximum or optimum group of member states respectively. These would jointly realise what the entirety of member states does not seem to be able to obtain, and, even so, raise the effectiveness of the whole system. As in those gradation concepts which favour integration, the basic approach of differentiated integration is to be understood as a conditional approach – as a rescue operation in case of the European Union's paralysis or collapse as a result of overstretching. The more capable of, and favourable towards, integration the entirety of the member states is, the less differentiation will be needed.

In the process of eastern enlargement, the first objective of a strategy for differentiated integration is to keep the European internal market, and the legal community grown around it, undivided under the shelter of the European Community. For this field, differentiation rules along the principle of graduated integration apply – basically by way of the previously successful practice of creating exceptions for new joining members for

---

[95] Cf., inter alia, Centre for Economic Policy Research (CEPR): Flexible Integration: Towards a More Effective and Democratic Europe, London 1995; Club von Florenz (ed.): Europa: Der unmögliche Status quo, Baden-Baden 1996; Janning, Josef: Europa braucht verschiedene Geschwindigkeiten, in: Europa-Archiv No. 18, 1994, pp. 527–536.
[96] Cf. Mertel, Michael/Prill, Norbert: Der verhängnisvolle Irrtum des Entweder-Oder – eine Vision für Europa, in: Frankfurter Allgemeine Zeitung of 19 July 1989.

a limited period of time. This prevents the present state of organisation from being softened into an elevated form of free-trade zone. It also binds full EU membership to being capable of participating in the internal market.

The second aim is to realise a common currency as well as a common defence, even in an enlarging European Union. These steps would now be made by those member states which would be ready, and able, to do so – if necessary, based on special agreements. Their design ought to allow for an enlargement along clearly defined rules; only participating member states should have the right to cooperate. Institutions concerned with coordination and cooperation, which support combined efforts of the core groups with the remaining parts of the Union, should, therefore, be further developed.

As regards economic and monetary union, the Maastricht Treaty has already envisaged that the progress of those member states meeting the requirements for participation will not be subject to any deadlines – all other member states will subsequently be expected also to fulfil the stability criteria and join the union. Differentiated integration is based on the assumption that these periods will be considerably longer in the big European Union, some member states will fail to fulfil the stability criteria in the long term, and others would not be able to join even though they fulfilled the criteria. Under these circumstances, monetary union remains as reasonable for the participating states as for those EU members which are oriented towards stability but do not belong to the common monetary region. Two complementary steps are necessary in order to ensure differentiated monetary integration: firstly, those states which are the first to form monetary union should agree on binding basic rules which make sure that the criteria for entering monetary union remain valid.[97] This would efficiently guarantee that wrong behaviour could afterwards be sanctioned, a possibility laid down in the contract. Secondly, the members of monetary union ought to contribute the stability weight of their common currency to a renewed European Monetary System with adjusted margins so as to support the stabilisation policy of non-partici-

---

97 This is also the starting point of the Stability Pact for Europe, suggested by the Federal Minister of Finance, Waigel. Cf. the text of this initiative, published in Agence Europe of 24 November 1995.

pating member states. Thus the Central and Eastern European member states would additionally be granted a soft transition into the stability conditions of monetary integration.

A differentiated concept for European security

In the field of common defence policy and common defence, the Maastricht treaty does not provide similar rules. The group of full members of the Western European Union has already been too heterogeneous; defence union within the framework of differentiated integration should therefore be based on a separate set of agreements.[98] This defence union would integrate the existing combined arms units of its members; promote the development of European structures and military infrastructure by concentrating its own means; provide the framework so that French and British nuclear weapons have a function with a view to Europe; and show security pledges of the EU. At any rate, basically each member of the European Union must have the possibility to take part; but more consistently than has previously been the case in this field in the EU and the WEU, participation must be bound to the capacity to, and readiness for, common defence. Similar to the field of monetary union, defence union ought to cooperate closely with an advanced Common Foreign and Security Policy (CFSP). This means that member states united in defence union should, as a whole, be part of the CFSP, and they ought to join forces in order to contribute to the decisions made within its framework. The CFSP could thus also be opened for an early membership of candidates.

Moreover, a differentiated defence union could resolve the enlarged European Union's security dilemma: on the one hand, equal, indivisible security has been one of the unwritten bases of the contract underlying the integration process since its beginnings in the 1950s – at first with regard to the security from each other, afterwards with regard to the non-military aspects of security in a wider sense. Annulling this implicit promise in

---

98 Cf. Weidenfeld, Werner/Janning, Josef: The new Europe. Strategies for differentiated integration, Presentation at the International Bertelsmann Forum on the Petersberg on 19–20 January 1996.

case of an enlarged European Union seems hardly consistent with the logic of the internal market, economic and monetary union or the Common Foreign and Security Policy. If, on the other hand, the Europeans do not develop a visible defence capacity, they will not manage to make their interpretation of the Atlantic Alliance a binding one: the Alliance would be a "community of democracies", in which all democracies on the European continent could find their place if they desired it. Membership of the European Union is combined with the invitation also to join the Western European Union, with all its rights and obligations. If the ties between the EU, the WEU and NATO are to be maintained, on principle nothing else can apply to these states' membership of NATO, notwithstanding the fact that all member states of the alliance are required to agree. The United States and the other NATO members will share this view, all the more so if all full members of the WEU are also full members of NATO.

The future Europe will comprise net payers and net receivers in the field of external security. By integrating Scandinavia and East Central Europe, the EU itself will become Russia's neighbour and share the risks of this situation with Finland or Poland, for example. The danger of a renaissance of the Soviet Union and its imperial pretensions continues to be a residual risk, which is difficult to calculate, but hardly probable, even though the Slavic republics were reintegrated into the CIS. This additional responsibility and power will be too much for some of the present and future members. Hardly any of the security institutions is keyed in such a way that a group of European states jointly, visibly and credibly could undertake to play this part and form a defence union.

To date, however, quite a lot is started by way of ad-hoc coalitions so that preventive diplomacy can hardly unfold itself effectively. How European defence efforts are really connected to the different institutional points of reference, remains indistinct. By contrast, the Europeans are groping their way between renationalisation, NATO reform and the renaissance of the WEU towards new structures in a way which leaves all options open, thus leaving many issues undecided. The reform steps of the next years must start here by clarifying responsibilities of the EU, the WEU and NATO and forming an institutional framework capable to act, in which decisions can also be made by the majority, and implemented by those member states which are willing to act.

For that purpose, European policy must first of all organise its foreign and security-policy interests in such a way that they are effectively represented. The Common Foreign and Security Policy ought to be consistently developed further on the basis of the following priorities. It should:
– give priority to the European Union when it comes to assigning responsibility in the policy towards Eastern Europe, in Mediterranean policy, development policy, OSCE and UN policy; and bind the member states in their national foreign policy to be loyal to the Union;
– introduce a protective clause similar to article 5 of the NATO Treaty into the contractual framework of the Common Foreign and Security Policy;
– push ahead the formulation of common positions with regard to principles, criteria and objectives of the Union policy in these fields; based on these positions subsequent decisions will be made by the majority, or at least by way of positive abstention;
– develop a suitable foreign-policy infrastructure, which also permits permanently to evaluate the situation in the light of common interests and brings the resources of the European Commission and the Western European Union together;
– assign the Western European Union as defensive arm to the European Union and put it in charge of the planning and realisation of military details of foreign and security-policy decisions. Moreover, based on basic EU rulings, full members of the WEU should be given the opportunity to employ their own means and take military action on behalf of the Union.

In addition, a differentiated approach is suitable to merge the defence institutions presently just existing alongside each other into a system of western security which takes the security of both America and Europe into account. The obvious idea is to instal several levels:
– On the European level the Western European Union would organise integrated territorial defence. Its planning and leadership structures would be compatible with those of NATO.
– As European part of the Atlantic Alliance, the WEU concentrates its member states' resources and obligations within the framework of NATO.
– In order to reinsure the Alliance, nuclear deterrence would be guaran-

teed by the United States on the American side, and Great Britain and France on the European side.

This pragmatic strategy divides the large European Union's problems of control into different fields. When it comes to putting differentiated integration into practice, negative consequences (institutional fragmentation of a Europe à la carte, decision-making processes becoming even more intricate) are hardly to be apprehended. Differentiation is focused on two clearly defined political spheres with substantial prerequisites for entry, the institutional structure of which can have a very simple design depending on the convergence conditions. In the sphere of the Union these core units will often appear as "caucuses" with well-prepared positions of consensus and joint initiatives, thus contributing to eliminating confusion in a Union of 27 member states. Differentiating integration according to this pattern will considerably contribute to the large EU's governability, as it accompanies enlargement by a specific deepening process, and offers efficient member states incentives for integrating their resources. In practice, moreover, the leader function within the EU would focus on those member states which, to a certain extent, form the intersection of different areas of integration, i.e. which fully participate in all fields of integration.

2. The Balkans: stabilising peace

Although the international community has committed itself on a large scale in the Balkans since the war in Yugoslavia started, the risks to peace in the region have not yet decreased. An adequate *Ostpolitik* towards the Balkans must therefore concentrate the efforts on securing peace. In order to promote the necessary politico-institutional change, framework conditions in terms of security policy must be guaranteed, and the instruments and concepts of the EU's policy are to be improved. Secondly, the causes fostering a violent escalation of ethnic contrasts must be taken into consideration: deficits due to a lack of modernisation in the fields of history, culture, economic and social structures as well as dysfunctions of the political systems. For this purpose, cooperation and negotiation processes must be organised, and the Balkan countries' development with regard to civil society and economy is to be supported.

Linking border guarantees and renunciation-of-violence guarantees

Diverging cultural identities and territorial fragmentation favour ethnic conflicts in the Balkans and destabilise the existing states. Both effects aggravate each other. The causes of this mechanism can only be eliminated by an extensive institutional change, by which a civil society can develop in the Balkan region. In order to start and support such a change, present borders must not be changed, and all actors must renounce the use of violence. The present borders are not maintained because they reflect historical justice or make up for historical injustice, but because there are no better alternatives for dividing the territory. Due to the ethnic fragmentation of the Balkans, new minorities would inevitably be created if minority territories seceded. An internationally approved border revision would, moreover, serve as a model for other border conflicts in the Balkans and all over Eastern Europe. The mere option for a border revision would already encourage the individual parties to increase the gravity of the conflict by concentrating on ethnic issues. Therefore territorial exchange is also hardly recommendable: it has occasionally been taken into consideration; the Federal Republic of Yugoslavia, for example, would thus be offered the Republic of Bosnian Serbs in exchange for Kosovo. In correspondence with the traditional position of the UN, state sovereignty and the continued existence of international borders should be given priority over the right to self-determination.

Governments must not be enabled to abuse state sovereignty for the discrimination of minorities. Basing state borders not on controversial principles of historic (or ethnic) justice but on the status quo might be considered illegitimate. For these reasons, it must be guaranteed that all intra-state political actors renounce the use of violence in settling their conflicts. Therefore a legal basis which enables neutral parties to interfere must be clearly defined; in contrast to the traditional position of international law this legal basis to be established would also refer to domestic use of violence constituting offences against human rights (e. g. far-reaching police operations against ethnic minorities). The CSCE Helsinki Document of July 1992 providing peace-keeping operations of the CSCE in national conflicts ought to be worked out and formalised for this purpose. A multilateral institution, such as the OSCE or the UN, must establish whether, and to what extent, human and minority rights are violated. Depending on the results of this monitoring, corresponding sanctions, and even military intervention (peace enforcement), must be applied. Intervention requires a political mandate, which the OSCE or the UN Security Council would be able to grant. In order to prevent blockades within the OSCE, institutionalising a functioning "European Security Council" within the framework of the OSCE would make sense (cf. chapter IV.3).

Legitimation on the multilateral level is needed so that individual states or federations cannot be empowered to employ the ban on violence, which restricts state sovereignty, in order to succeed with possible hegemonic interests. NATO must not enforce a renunciation-of-violence guarantee without a mandate. Arguments here are therefore in favour of a system of collective security and against security concepts based on the supremacy of one actor.[99] The strategy suggested includes two methods which make the collective security concept less vulnerable: border guarantees and renunciation-of-violence guarantees are made subject to conditions which are as objective as possible; and these guarantees are embedded in an extensive strategy for peace, which prevents attempts at ethnic mobilisation. The advantage of a renunciation-of-violence guarantee is that the western democracies or the EU need not internationalise (and thus aggravate) national ethnic conflicts in order to preserve possibilities to intervene.[100] In addition, within the framework of the trilateral security partnership with the USA and Europe yet to be established, Russia can thus be integrated into all stages of conflict-handling. For Bosnia-Herzegovina this means that the SFOR troops, which guarantee the re-

---

99 Cf. Czempiel, Ernst-Otto: Die Neuordnung Europas. Was leisten NATO und OSZE für die Kooperation mit Osteuropa und Rußland, in: Aus Politik und Zeitgeschichte 1–2/1997. By contrast cf. Rühl, Lothar: Lehren für die NATO aus der Bosnien-Intervention. Eine vorläufige Bilanz aus westlicher Sicht, Neue Zürcher Zeitung of 2 April 1996.
100 Oeter, Stefan: Bosnien und Europa – ein Unfall der Völkerrechtsordnung?, in: Stefanov, Nenad/ Werz, Michael (eds.): Bosnien und Europa. Die Ethnisierung der Gesellschaft, Frankfurt 1995.

nunciation of violence in the country, remain stationed as long as the parties involved might again resort to violence when pursuing their interests. The EU ought to advocate that the mandate is correspondingly designed. In its relations with the USA the EU should point to the risks of a policy which tries to substitute the international community's security guarantees by developing parity of military powers. In a parallel process the Western European Union must be given the operative means, and thus be enabled to carry out independently peace-keeping and peace-enforcement operations on behalf of the UN or the OSCE.

Border guarantees and renunciation-of-violence guarantees must be credible, based on an exact evaluation of the situation, and consist of graded measures. Peace-keeping operations in which international units are permitted to deploy military force merely in order to defend themselves are reasonable only to a certain degree of escalation.[101] They should, in the future, be organised and equipped in such a way that, if necessary, their mandate can be enlarged to peace enforcement which would allow for their employing military force in order to push through the mandate. Conflict management must, moreover, take into consideration that the ethnic conflicts and areas of tension in the Balkans are interdependent in more than one respect: in Bosnia-Herzegovina the parties at war imitated their opponents' successful strategies, and the Bosnian Serbs' strategy for founding their state could become a model for other ethnic minorities. The actors compare the policies of the USA, the EU and other international organisations and try to play them off against each other. Furthermore, grave consequences for other areas of conflicts could quickly result from a regional escalation.

Flexible and graduated cooperation

In future the EU must make considerable efforts to solve the problems of coordinating its Balkan policy. In order to achieve this, a system of rules is necessary which links the different stages of political and eco-

---

101 Cf. Taroor, Shashi: The Role of the United Nations in European Peacekeeping, in: Chayes, Abram/ Handler Chayes, Antonia (eds.): Preventing Conflict in the Post-Communist World. Mobilizing International and Regional Organizations, Washington 1996.

nomic cooperation with the Balkan states to clear-cut conditions. These conditions, their fulfilment and the EU measures thus to be triggered off must form a flexible, graduated régime of cooperation and integration. This régime has to be plausible and calculable for the Balkan states, its stages would be reversible, i. e. in order to sanction failures, it would be possible to go back on them. The rules should become binding for the EU member states, i. e. they should be formulated as Common Position and enforced as Common Action. Thus the member states would have to orientate their national foreign policies closely to the Union's foreign policy. Moreover, the regional approach, initiated by the EU after the conclusion of the Dayton accords, ought to be further developed.[102]

The present regional approach is based on linking EU cooperation with the countries of the former Yugoslavia with the states' own cooperation efforts. In order to conclude trade and cooperation agreements with the EU, the states concerned will thus have to contribute to the consolidation of peace and respect human and minority rights as well as democratic principles. Furthermore the economic cooperation provided for in the trade and cooperation agreements will depend on the individual states' cooperating with their neighbours. This means that they will have to design mutual measures to promote the free trade of goods, persons and services and develop joint projects. However, the EU must make it even clearer to the governments of the Balkan countries that it does not intend to reinstate Yugoslavia, but that being willing to cooperate on good-neighbourly terms is an essential prerequisite for the long-term integration into the internal market of the EU.

In terms of concept, the Balkan policy of the EU is to be improved in two directions. Firstly, beyond trade and cooperation agreements the Balkan countries should get a clear perspective of EU association and membership. This ought to be combined with general normative obligations and specific programmes for the development of democracy. There is no convincing argument in favour of excluding the Balkan states from EU membership in the long run. In principle, it seems to be reasonable

---

[102] Cf. the conclusions of the EU's foreign ministers of 10 December 1995 and 26 February 1996 (Agence Europe of 27 March 1996) as well as the report of the Commission KOM (96) 252, Brussels 1996.

further to differentiate the stages of cooperation in such a way as is endeavoured with the sui-generis agreement suggested for Albania. This would improve the instruments by which the EU directs national democratisation and liberalisation programmes.[103]

Conjuring up far-away aims like democracy and peace is not sufficient. They are desirable in the Western European context, but due to the lack of basic conditions they have merely symbolic significance in the Balkans. By contrast, the EU should direct all available resources to promoting cooperation between the actors on different levels with partial, but feasible objectives, and to improving mutual trust. More is needed here than just the activities until now provided for by the "process for stability and good neighbourhood in Southeast Europe", which is part of the regional approach. Rather than convincing the actors that cooperation is indeed useful, the most important aim of this process is to establish stable conditions for the actors' negotiations and directive efforts. A multilateral framework should be built, in which governments and non-government organisations of the Balkan states can regularly convene in order to negotiate solutions to their problems.

If the EU tries to relieve the process by which stability and good neighbourhood are to be established by leaving border and minority issues out of consideration, it avoids the central problems of the region. Apart from the fact that the unsolved core problems will make it difficult to come to an agreement about other questions, or even obstruct it, this strategy seems to be too defensive, when compared with the ordering design of the Dayton agreement. Instead, the EU should follow the model of the stability pact more closely and initiate bilateral agreements between neighbour states, which give a border guarantee and simultaneously grant minorities rights to self-government. Its authority ought, moreover, help to bring institutional mechanisms of settling minority problems on the agenda of talks between the Balkan states.

In terms of security and foreign policy, the challenges in the Balkans require more efficient decision-making structures within the EU itself

---

[103] In its guidelines for the future relations of the EU with Albania, the EU Commission pleaded for concluding an agreement sui generis, which would go beyond the trade and cooperation agreement of 1992 and enable Albania to participate in the approximation strategy. However, this agreement would not have the dimensions of an association agreement. Cf. Agence Europe of 29 January 1996.

and in the relations between the EU and other international organisations. The division of tasks and roles between the EU, the Council of Europe and the OSCE should be further developed (cf. chapter V.1). The OSCE as an instrument of preventive diplomacy could take over monitoring and mediating functions in the Balkans; the Council of Europe could concentrate on developing the European norms of the protection of human rights and minorities. The function of the OSCE would then mainly be to manage ethnic problems in the Balkan countries, whereas the Council of Europe would have to inspect the quality. Closely interlinked with these institutions, the EU should more intensively act the part of political and economic centre of attraction, i. e. function as anchor of modernisation and stability and form the multi-level system of integration. Secondly, the EU must adopt qualified majority vote as decision-making principle within the CFSP. Within the sharing of tasks with the organisations of the Council of Europe and the OSCE, which are intergovernmentally characterised, it would then be able to deal more efficiently with its role as supranational institution towards the Balkan states. It would also prevent blockades by individual EU member states, thus exerting a certain pressure on the governments to form coalitions and clarify common interests. Reinforcing the majority principle in the CFSP is the most important prerequisite to ensure that the suggested system of flexible and graduated cooperation in the EU's Balkan policy functions in the long run.

Coping with minority problems

The ethnic conflicts are mainly caused by various political groups' not being tolerant enough as regards ethnic differences in the Balkan states. By granting border guarantees the EU (or the international community respectively) would exclude that conflicts are settled by a secession of ethnic minorities or a separation of states. In order to transform security based on a military fundament into political stability, it is necessary to settle the minority problems within the existing states. As it is capable of combining its strategy for cooperation with a country-related policy which aims at democratisation and decentralisation, the EU has the relevant instruments at its disposal. Problems in the individual conflict areas could be tackled as follows:[104]

Within the framework of the process encouraging stability and good neighbourhood in Southeast Europe, relations between Albania and the FRY and Macedonia with their Albanian minorities should be stabilised by bilateral basic treaties. The conclusion of such treaties ought to be made a prerequisite for an EU Association Agreement with Albania. The stability effect of these treaties would be that Albania acknowledges the integrity of the borders of both countries. The FRY would, in turn, give concrete autonomy rights to the Kosovo-Albanians; Macedonia would commit itself to grant more protective rights and rights of co-determination to the Albanian minority. Croatia and the FRY must first of all acknowledge each other. Secondly, the EU should initiate a bilateral agreement which declares both states' territorial integrity and settles open conflicts and the rights of the Serbian minority in East Slavonia. At the same time, the governments of these countries must understand that such an agreement would have to be concluded before they could be associated with the EU.

For Bosnia-Herzegovina a multi-ethnic coexistence, which is indeed an objective of the Dayton agreement, may well seem to be politically desirable. However, due to the war there is so much bitterness and hatred among the individual population groups that nationalist politicians can still mobilise people. Therefore it seems impossible at present to rebuild multi-ethnic settlement areas. The rigid schedule of the Dayton accords ignores the time needed for a politico-cultural change; the multi-ethnic ordering concept will thus be provoked to fail. The international commitment should be guided by whether the political, social and human rights situation in Bosnia-Herzegovina consolidates itself, and not by the agenda of American domestic politics. A realistic strategy for Bosnia, which would be scheduled for the long term, will also be able to accept that the country is de facto divided into Bosniak, Serb and Croat settlement areas – as long as the borders of Bosnia-Herzegovina remain intact and the

---

104 Cf. also the detailed recommendations in: International Commission on the Balkans: Unfinished Peace. Report of the International Commission on the Balkans, Washington 1996; Rubin, Barnett R. (ed.): Towards Comprehensive Peace in Southeast Europe. Conflict Prevention in the South Balkans, New York 1996; Calic, Marie-Janine (ed.): Friedenskonsolidierung im ehemaligen Jugoslawien: Sicherheitspolitische und zivile Aufgaben, SWP S 413, Ebenhausen 1996.

country will be prevented from disintegrating. Such a division will be legitimate if it is bound to a strategy which improves the framework conditions of civil society and economy in the individual ethnic areas, thus promoting interest in a non-ethnic mode of politics and reintegration.

The EU policy towards the FRY needs a new concept. The EU has never clearly linked acknowledgement of the FRY up with the approval of human and minority rights. It has wavered between three positions: the FRY should acknowledge all successor states of the former Yugoslavia, i. e. Croatia just as well as Macedonia; the FRY should merely acknowledge Macedonia and respect human and minority rights; or acknowledging Macedonia would be enough for the FRY.[105] Ultimately, most EU member states have already re-established diplomatic relations with the FRY after Macedonia was acknowledged. Precise conditions for the FRY's membership of the OSCE and the Council of Europe should now be laid down. According to a decision made in Cannes in June 1995, the European Council was to reintegrate the FRY into the international community, provided that the minority questions in the FRY developed "satisfactorily", though this wording is rather imprecise. The terms for eventual acknowledgement have not been expressed in a more precise form, either.

In order to make these conditions more concrete, the EU should consult independent Serb academics and international experts on the Balkans and jointly design a coherent concept for a more far-reaching federalisation of the FRY. The basic idea underlying this concept ought to be that Vojvodina, Sandzak and Kosovo receive the same status as the Republic of Montenegro. On the one hand, responsibilities and resources must be decentralised as fully as possible; on the other hand, effective mechanisms of co-determination are to be established on the federal level. Implementing these regulations must be made a prerequisite of membership of the OSCE and the Council of Europe and of EU association. Moreover, the OSCE missions in Vojvodina, Sandzak and Kosovo, whose mandate the FRY did not prolong in June 1993, ought to be resumed immediately.[106] Their re-establishment is to be demanded before the FRY's integration into the OSCE will be further negotiated.

---

105 Cf. Agence Europe of 29/30 and 31 January 1996.
106 Cf. Schmidt, Fabian: The Sandzak: Muslims between Serbia and Montenegro, in: RFE/RL Research Report, 11 February 1994.

When it comes to stabilising relations in the Balkans, the EU member state Greece and the associated CEE states Bulgaria, Romania, Slovenia and Hungary as regional neighbours are given a special task. These countries should develop forms of regional cooperation on all levels and function as stabilising centres. The EU could, for example, call upon the associated states of Southeast Europe to let individual Balkan governments join in the "structured dialogue" with the EU. Greece and the associated states of the region could also start a regional dialogue with a view to EU integration. Upon Greek initiative, relations between Albania and Greece started normalising in March 1995; and the interim agreement between Greece and Macedonia also shows that such initiatives are possible. The EU could grant special PHARE funds for such initiatives; and it should insofar extend the regional approach to the Central and Eastern European association states as their endeavours at regional cooperation are made a prerequisite for their further integration into the EU.

In terms of conflict prevention, the situation must be improved in a process which runs simultaneously to this country-related policy:

– In ethnic conflicts international attemps at mediation must start as soon as possible. The OSCE, the EU and the Council of Europe will here have to offer their know-how; their duty will also be to deal with the psychological-social backgrounds of the conflict. They should, however, not bind the different parties to prefabricated solutions. Moreover, individual regulations of international law must be made more precise. All member states of the Council of Europe should, for example, ratify the Framework Convention on National Minorites, and the European Convention on Human Rights should be supplemented by a protocol on the cultural rights of persons belonging to national minorities.

– Bit by bit, NATO ought to integrate all states of the former Yugoslavia into its "Partnership for Peace" programme. By making use of the consultation mechanisms provided by PfP, it would contribute to building up confidence in the military field.

– Talks on arms control and disarmament between Bosnia-Herzegovina, Croatia and the FRY must be seen in context with the external border and renunciation-of-force guarantees. This means that talks should not only be orientated on producing parity of forces, but also go one step further and concentrate on substantially diminishing military potentials.

Economic development

Growing economic integration with the EU would support the liberal, western-oriented élites of the Balkan countries in their attemps at societal modernisation. The EU should, in the first place, back private-enterprise economic links and integration of the region, since they promote interest in transnational cooperation and politico-social stability in the long run. Economic aid, association agreements and prospects for integration are important instruments which can help to eliminate the causes of ethnic conflicts. In addition, they can be applied in political negotiations to support demands for democratic and constitutional principles. However, the possibilities to support democratisation processes by politico-economic sanctions ought not to be overestimated. The economic systems of the Balkan countries have not yet been sufficiently integrated into the region and into world economy. In consequence, the effects of external economic incentives or sanctions are limited.[107] In addition, the persisting agricultural structures and the shadow economy will further offer non-cooperative political élites alternative possibilities to evade any sanctions.

The EU has already concluded trade and cooperation agreements with Albania and Macedonia. Similar agreements are planned with Croatia, Bosnia-Herzegovina and the FRY. At the conference on Bosnia held in London in December 1995, the EU Commission held out the prospect of medium-term association to the former Yugoslav states. The EU acted quickly, mainly as far as reconstruction in Bosnia-Herzegovina was concerned: it was the first international organisation to make funds available.[108] This flexibility and efficiency must be maintained for the recon-

---

107 Cf., however, Reuter, Jens: Die Wirtschaft der BR Jugoslawien nach der Suspendierung der Sanktionen, in: Südosteuropa Vol. 45, 8/1996.
108 In 1996 the EU gave US$ 373 m for the reconstruction of lodging and infrastructure in Bosnia-Herzegovina. In 1996 the international community made funds amounting to a total of US$ 1.8 bn available.

struction tasks of years to come. The EU should mainly concentrate on the following measures:
- Modernising agriculture in the Balkan region is most urgently needed; it is closely connected to the opening of export chances. Cooperation and association agreements must, therefore, not be restricted by protectionist interests of the EU states. Even though the Commission guaranteed preferential entry for industrial products from the successor states of Yugoslavia, it wants to make import concessions for agricultural products dependent on the specific preconditions of individual markets. This reservation must not be used by European agricultural organisations to enforce protectionist measures, which would endanger economic modernisation in the Balkans.
- Besides Albania, Bosnia-Herzegovina and Macedonia, the other states of the former Yugoslavia should also be integrated into the PHARE programme. The PHARE programme must be suitably restructured. Previous experience shows that funds must be primarily spent in the countries themselves; in line with local priorities they should also be invested in infrastructure.
- In addition, the London-based European Bank for Reconstruction and Development (EBRD) ought to shift its commitment from the more successful Central and Eastern European states, in which foreign private banks have meanwhile made capital available, not only to the CIS states, but also to the Balkan countries. Their capital market is still underdeveloped. The focus should be placed on the newly developing private-enterprise sector. Moreover, the EBRD ought to cooperate mainly with local commercial and development banks, offer interest subsidies for loans to domestic small and medium-sized businesses and support trade relations between EU and Balkan companies by export guarantees.
- The EU's PHARE programme and Joint-Venture-PHARE programme (JOPP) should be made increasing use of in order to improve the framework conditions for foreign investors in the Balkans. Foreign direct investment will be indispensable if the region is to undergo economic modernisation.[109] Round table talks between EU companies and en-

---

109 Until June 1995 the cumulated per-capita foreign investment in Albania, Croatia and Macedonia, which was just under US$ 30, made up only one-seventh of the corresponding amount in the Visegrád states. Cf. UN-ECE: Economic Bulletin for Europe Vol. 47, 1995, p. 104.

terprises or administrative units in the Balkan countries should form the starting point for well-aimed investment promotion.
- The EU has made it a prerequisite for cooperation with a Balkan country that markets for goods, persons and services are bilaterally liberated. The process of liberalisation must be further developed. Within the framework of cooperation structures a regional free-trade zone in the Balkans should be particularly supported.
- Ultimately, programmes to fight structural poverty and unemployment are required. Programmes for professional qualification, assistance given to company establishments and a politico-economic strategy to support the existing potential in the individual regions ought to be linked together.

Strengthening civil society

The EU must promote a politico-cultural transformation in the region in order to change the prerequisites of politics in the Balkans. This transformation cannot be achieved by binding contracts of individual governments. It is, on the contrary, a process right up from below, which results from numerous decisions and changes of behaviour of individual persons. Market economy and democracy cannot be introduced from the top; they depend on whether the citizens become active entrepreneurs and participate in political proceedings. Only then will civic, instead of ethnic, concepts of nations have a chance to persist. In this regard, distinct concepts are needed further to develop the "process of stability and good neighbourhood in the southeast of Europe" initiated by the EU.

Strengthening civil societies is all the more important since the development in Central and Eastern Europe shows that real transformation of system is a gradual process, in which a professional-technocratic mode of thinking steadily prevails. The governing élites part with their political power. Instead, they orientate themselves exclusively on economic criteria and interests.[110] In the Balkan region the shaping of political will

110 Szelényi, Iván/Szelényi, Szonja: Circulation or Reproduction of Élites during the Post-Communist Transformation in Eastern Europe, in: Theory and Society Vol. 24, 1995, pp. 615–638.

and decision-making processes can thus be rationalised. The danger of populism and instability can be lessened.

In order to induce professional value orientation of élites and changes in the patterns of behaviour, the EU must, to a higher extent than before, support individual centres of civic culture and modernisation in the Balkans. Such centres can be represented by governments, parties, media, employers' associations, churches or other non-government organisations. On different levels, societal initiatives are to be interwoven, rather than supporting centralised forms of cooperation in dependence on individual governments. Civil-society connections would, particularly in the FRY, render politics more flexible. The international community could thus make use of economic sanctions and measures of political outlawing, while at the same time keeping in touch with society's players. The following individual measures are to be realised:

– Consultation and training programmes for the political and administrative élites should be developed so as to prevent ethnic conflicts and successfully deal with conflict situations.
– Cross-border professional networks (such as trade associations, trade unions, youth organisations) are to be promoted and reinforced by multilateral PHARE programmes in the individual countries.
– The educational systems and investment in the educational sector of the Balkan states must be developed in order to support professional, open-minded élites.
– Cross-border economic interests ought to be promoted so that an economic lobby, interested in cooperation and trade, can organise itself in the Balkans.
– Dialogue between the different churches and denominations must be initiated; it should aim at concluding a charter on principles of tolerance and common interests, thus depriving nationalist politicians of an important basic argument.
– Modelled on the American station "Radio Free Europe", an independent Serbocroat TV and radio programme is to be established, as has already been initiated by the administration of the High Representative of the UN for Bosnia-Herzegovina.
– Societal interests must be linked; in addition, the EU countries' interests in, and potentials of, a transfer of cooperation and know-how are

to be mobilised. Besides humanitarian-charitable action, decentralised forms of specialist exchange and partnerships for development should be supported. The refugees from former Yugoslavia and those persons from the Balkan countries who migrated in search of work could take on an important mediating function on this level.
- A refugee policy which aims at deporting persons as quickly as possible into an uncertain future must be abandoned. Young refugees from Bosnia should rather undergo professional training in the receiving states; this would be financed by loans and bound to their return to Bosnia.

A coherent EU foreign policy is very important. There are, however, numerous other levels within the European Union on which cooperation and integration take place. These must also be employed in order to cooperate with the Balkan countries. The EU's task is to break up the public's hardened indifference and rouse an interest in the region which is not fixated on exploding ethnic violence. Making the Balkans less peripheral in terms of culture, economy and politics must be the foremost aim. Against this background, granting prospects for integration would not only be important for the region, but also for the European public. There is still a need to communicate that the public's perception of the Balkans is limited, and that the region has a future beyond ethnic wars and conflicts. This future is represented by European cooperation and a long-term integration into the future all-European context.

3. Russia and the CIS: partnership and cooperation

A scenario of new proximity and neighbourhood in a converging Europe is the starting point of the policy towards Russia and the CIS. Opening western structures to the east will create new dependences, but also new and often overlapping interests. All sides must consider this future neighbourhood as a chance rather than a risk, and they must develop the basis of a common partnership and security agenda. In terms of foreign policy an enlarged European Union's foreign-policy capacity to act will not least be decided by its dealing with Russia and the CIS. One of the most important all-Europan duties is to design a coherent and long-term *Ostpolitik*. It might become the catalyst of the developing European Common Foreign and Security Policy.

The partnership and cooperation agreements concluded with the leading CIS members, as well as the "Action Plans" for Russia and Ukraine, which in many respects are but letters of intent, must be further developed in important areas.[111] Preferential treatment, which is included in the clause on a free-trade agreement, must be specifically extended in the case of Russia and the European CIS members Belarus and Ukraine, which would already become direct neighbours of the EU after a first round of eastern enlargement. Basically, the principle of equal treatment must be upheld for these countries (and, in the long term, also for Moldavia). The development of Russia's western CIS neighbours as independent and stable states will be an important basis of the future European peace order. It is of major importance to include these three countries into a network of a trilateral security partnership, integrating the USA and based on NATO and the OSCE.[112]

Future cooperation must be based on a redefinition of common security interests, which by far exceed merely military threat scenarios. These interests include conflict prevention and settlement, the fight against international terrorism and drug trafficking, migration, infrastructure and energy issues as well as preventive measures in the nuclear and ecological fields. These interests should be fixed in a binding trilateral framework convention (including the USA, the EU and the three European CIS states). This should be based on the definition of common principles and obligations, such as those fixed in UN and OSCE documents. Human rights, the principle of free alliance and territorial integrity as well as compliance with international treaties are to be acknowledged.

The EU and NATO have the common task to combine integration with

---

111 Cf. also Annex, table 2: State of the partnership and cooperation agreements with Russia and the CIS.
112 A first concept for a trilateral agreement (involving Russia) is proposed by Graham Allison, Karl Kaiser and Sergei Karaganov: Hin zu einer neuen Gemeinschaft demokratischer Nationen, in: Internationale Politik No. 11 1996, pp. 1–6.

cooperation. Both processes must in future be better coordinated. For that purpose, full-time coordinators for Russia and the CIS ought to be appointed by the EU, but also in individual EU member states. To start with, the European CIS strategy ought to be concentrated on the above-mentioned risks and challenges. Thus democracy and market economy in the future European CIS neighbour states must further be supported; the post-Soviet territory must be internationally integrated; coordinated programmes guaranteeing nuclear and ecological security are required.

Aiding democracy and freedom of the media

Despite possible setbacks, the West must adhere to the aim of a democratisation of Russia and the western CIS republics. Peaceful internal stabilisation is a precondition for a cooperative foreign policy. The West must not be directed by wishful thinking nor by old threat reflections. The West has only limited opportunities for influence, but these must be used. A few principles are to be taken into account:
– The West must expect longer transition periods. In the foreseeable future, neither Russia nor the other CIS states will become democratic constitutional states according to the western liberal example.
– The West must support processes rather than persons in the future. Representatives of a wide political and social spectrum, and in particular all reform-oriented forces, must be involved in the dialogue. This applies to Russia, but also, for example, to the hard-pressed oppositional forces in Belarus.
– The West is on a tightrope walk between granting trust in advance and covering risks. Offers of cooperation are to be linked to clear partnership criteria. The West has to show flexibility, and at the same time more political consistency.
– In principle, supporting processes in civil society and democracy requires complementary action programmes. Political promotion "from the top" must be complemented by initiatives "from the bottom".

On the highest political level the catalogue of principles covered by a future trilateral framework declaration will play a major role. The EU as European partner continues to be the most important coordinator of programmes for democratic support. Beyond the "Action Plans" for Russia and Ukraine, the European Union should fix contacts with Russia, Belarus and Ukraine on several specialised and ministerial levels within the framework of a "structured dialogue", such as has existed with the Central and Eastern European states since 1994. The consensus about common democratic objectives, fixed by the European Union in the partnership and cooperation agreements, must be unequivocally adhered to. Contacts with all three CIS countries must include a wide spectrum of political, regional and independent forces. The political conditionality should be supported by a stringent system of graded sanctions on all levels of an institutionalised dialogue. This applies, in particular, to Russia which, after the presidential elections, does no longer require special political treatment.

An equally important instrument is the Council of Europe. Russia's membership (since February 1996) can only be part of an offensive strategy to enforce democratic and humanitarian norms if Russia is urged to fulfil the obligations it has undertaken. To date, only slow progress has become manifest.[113] The planned monitoring system must in future be implemented more efficiently. An examination of the membership of Belarus, while remote at present, of the Council of Europe is to be based on the principle of equality with Russia. In the long term, however, the Council of Europe cannot continue to take on new members on the principle of granting trust in advance; it must demand that European norms are fulfilled before membership can be granted. Otherwise, the credibility of the western society's normative system will be at stake.

At the same time, a series of grassroot initiatives is needed. Town twinning programmes form the best framework for direct contacts on the economic, cultural and social level. Nevertheless, few new town twinnings have been concluded since the radical changes at the end of the 1980s. Approximately 90 percent out of about 700 partnerships between the West and the CIS states (a good 400 with Russia alone) date back to Soviet times.[114] The "City Twinning programme" of the EU Commis-

---

113 On the conditions connected with membership cf. Frankfurter Allgemeine Zeitung of 27 January 1996 and Neue Zürcher Zeitung of 27/28 January 1996.
114 Cf. material provided at the conference "German-Russian town twinnings" of the Deutsch-Russisches Forum (German-Russian Forum) in Bonn on 12/13 March 1996.

sion is an important step into the right direction. It should be extended to the three European CIS states.[115] At the same time, individual EU member states will have to give corresponding support.

The new media are a field which should be supported by non-government organisations (NGOs). The past years have shown that the media are the most important bearers of hope for further democratisation in all transformation countries.[116] Even though government intervention increases, in particular in Belarus, an unprecedented variety of opinion leaders has developed. As yet, all democratically oriented media depend to a large extent on old or new financiers or regional administrative structures. At the same time the new private TV stations play a key role. The young private media structures must be supported on all levels. Training and exchange programmes, technical assistance, know-how transfer, consulting in the field of media law etc. are important issues, which ought to involve wider sections of the population: results of opinion polls indicate that public comprehension of the media in Russia, Belarus and Ukraine – unlike in Central and Eastern Europeans – is still based on authoritarian principles.[117] Programmes for further education and exchange are also useful in the university and educational sector. Youth exchange is of particular importance. To date, a dialogue with representatives of the new post-Soviet generation has hardly begun. Joint efforts should aim at establishing a "European-Russian youth network", modelled on the Franco-German and Polish-German youth networks; in the long run, this should be extended to Belarus and Ukraine.

A consistent regionalisation of political, social and cultural contacts, mainly with Russia, will be decisive. The old and new élites, whose influence is steadily growing, must be involved in the "structured dialogue". The central power in Moscow must be continuously assured that the West does not try to promote separatist tendencies, but the development of a stable federalism on which an efficient and pluralist Russia must be based.

---

115 Cf. European Commission: Practical Guide to the Tacis City Twinning Programme, Brussels 1995.
116 For a detailed survey cf. Transition, 6 October 1995; cf. also SINUS Moscow: Die Kommunikationselite in Rußland 1995, Befragung des SINUS-Instituts im Auftrag der Friedrich-Ebert-Stiftung, Moscow Office, April-May 1995.
117 Connors, Stephen et al.: Differing Views on Government Control, in: Transition 6 October 1996, pp. 26 ff.

Investment and the opening of markets

The future of the three western successor states of the USSR cannot be guaranteed by external financial aid. The political leaderships must pursue consistent reform and modernisation policies, which can only partly be supported from the outside. Russia, in particular, must understand that, in the 21st century, its national security will not be guaranteed by military or territorial resources, but by its integration and self-assertion in the international markets.[118] Russia has to realise that political and economic reforms are interdependent: a Russia whose incalculable behaviour revives old fears will lose attraction as international economic partner.

The European CIS countries must do their share in order to set off self-supporting processes of growth and become more attractive investment locations. The list of challenges leaves only little leeway to anti-reformist forces: apart from securing long-term monetary stability, removing obstacles to investment and creating a minimum of legal security, it is urgent to develop a competition policy, enforce workable tax and bankruptcy laws and establish a functioning financial administration.

To a limited degree, international financial transfers can compensate for deficits and shifts in the structuring policies of Russia, Belarus and Ukraine. The IMF must consistently develop its role within this framework. The latest credit agreements concluded with Russia (the second largest in the history of the IMF) and Ukraine support the countries' macroeconomic stabilisation. However, the political conditions of the credit agreement with Russia – which include the option to suspend payment of individual tranches – remain problematic.[119] With another six percent economic slump in 1996, the Russian economy did once again not fulfil the macroeconomic conditions of the IMF. Although the IMF revised Russia's permissible budget deficit target upwards to pave the way for further tranche payments, the core friction remains unsolved.

---

118 Russia's return to the international capital market with a first successful Eurobond issue last November was a positive signal. This was accompanied by a marked improvement of its credit rating.
119 Höhmann, Hans-Hermann/Meier, Christian: Präsidentschaftswahlen in Rußland: Westliche Unterstützungsmaßnahmen im Vorfeld des ersten Wahlgangs, in: Aktuelle Analysen des BIOst No. 40, 1996.

Beyond possible suspensions or revisions of payment programmes, the IMF must in time develop a concept for its future policy towards Russia. Above all, the political pressure which has accompanied the most recent financial aid to Moscow is to be eased.

The World Bank, the European Bank for Reconstruction and Development (EBRD) and the TACIS programme of the EU should support structural reforms more strongly than before. In order to achieve this, regional expertise, which has continuously been lacking in all three institutions, must be developed. In order to make project-oriented assistance in the CIS states more efficient, the available evaluation potential has to be reinforced. Moreover, excessive bureaucracy and lacking transparency, which also obstruct the World Bank's activities in the CIS, are to be reduced rigorously.

On the other hand, the World Bank should in no way submit to Russian criticism of project-related loans for structural adaptation and reconstruction. The experience gained during the first stage of transformation clearly shows that only project-related financial aid can effectively contribute to modernising reform states. However, new perspectives have been opened up for Russia and the other CIS countries after the EBRD (in which the EU has a 51 percent share) decided to double the capital in 1996.[120] Activities are increasingly transferred to the poorer and less successful transformation states of the CIS, which is to be welcomed. Two principles should apply to assistance provided by TACIS and PHARE alike: technical obstacles and bureaucracy on the side of the EU must be reduced, while running times and funds must be increased within realistic limits. In addition, in the next project term provisions should be made for a significant part of the funds to be spent in the receiving country. All western actors should concentrate on the growing private sector as well as the energy and raw materials sector. For all European CIS states (where Russia is an exporter and Belarus and Ukraine are dependent importers), the latter is a strategic issue of survival, which requires considerable transfers of investment and know-how from abroad.

Besides public support, private investment is indispensable for all three CIS countries to recover economically. Although direct foreign invest-

---

120 Frankfurter Allgemeine Zeitung of 17 April 1996.

ment in Russia rose in 1995, the total value still remains dangerously low.[121] The conditions of the structuring policy in the reform countries will be decisive. Upon further developing the EU partnership agreements, the focus ought to be consistently placed on eliminating obstacles to investment. The West should reward successes by improving export support.[122] Establishing a "clearing agency" of the investing industry on the European level would be equally important. Modelled on the East-West Committee of German Industry, it could work as an important intermediary between western policy and the CIS partner states. Regional information forums, exhibitions and specialised bilateral working groups should be supported on the non-institutional level. Partnerships between chambers of commerce and industry, or trade respectively, such as exist between Moscow and Dusseldorf, would also be an important pillar.

A further opening of western markets is more decisive than all directive intervention. The motto for Russia and both its European CIS neighbour countries must be the same as for all transformation countries: trade rather than aid. The threatening development towards protectionist measures must be stopped. The new Russian export law, adopted at the end of 1995, has resulted in new tariff and non-tariff barriers for the import of foodstuffs, alcohol and textiles, and is leading into the wrong direction. The provisions of the EU partnership agreement, which grant Russian industry protective measures for a transition period, must immediately be spelt out more precisely. The EU itself could give a signal by reducing limitations on sensitive goods (steel, textiles), to which the European CIS states are subject. The EU should stop using anti-dumping regulations as protectionist instruments. Existing agreements should be examined or revised within the framework of the joint cooperation councils, and in coordination with the IMF, so as to avoid a worsening of relations and the possibility of an open "trade war".

In the long term the most important aim is a free-trade agreement between the EU and Russia, Belarus and Ukraine. This would open the

---

121 Altogether US$ 3.9 bn; compared to Hungary with approximately US$ 7.4 bn. The accumulated foreign direct investment in Belarus is estimated at merely US$ 40 m until June 1995. Cf. UN-ECE: ibd., p. 104.
122 The categories of the export credit guarantees provided by the German credit insurer Hermes, which have recently been upgraded, show that to date capacities have not been made full use of since there are no guarantees on the Russian side.

prospects for a vast free-trade area from the Atlantic to the Pacific. According to the formula laid down in the partnership and cooperation agreement with Russia, possibilities of entering into talks will not be examined before 1998. However, the West and the three European CIS states should, as early as today, go beyond this and jointly develop a concrete schedule, which could be adjusted, if need be.

Furthermore, it is important to accelerate the development of growing economic interdependence across future borders. The OECD countries must further reduce customs barriers and increase import quotas. A liberal trade policy remains the best basis to support that Russia, Ukraine, and in the long term Belarus, will be accepted into the World Trade Organisation (WTO). Membership of the WTO is the precondition for Russia's international integration and the most important basis for its integration into the G7 group.

Integration and cooperation in the new Europe

The gradual hardening of Russian foreign policy and the complex developments in the CIS require a differentiated western security strategy. Integration of the eastern neighbour states into an enlarged Europe should be supported by four pillars. The European Union, NATO, an enlarged international contact group and an OSCE strengthened by a "European Security Council", could together form a firm network of mutually reinforcing institutions, on which to build up the future European security architecture. Their respective specific tasks would be:

The European Union

As direct neighbour the EU is, more than before, given a key role when it comes to integrating Russia and the European CIS states into the political structures of the future Europe. The future Central and Eastern European member states must, in particular, be integrated early on into the *Ostpolitik* towards Russia and the CIS. Given that relations are to be deepened and internationalised, the EU must place the focus on the political dimension of the partnership. EU membership should in principle be open to Belarus, and notably to Ukraine, which is seeking it in the long term. In addition, Ukraine ought to be offered an associated status (without automatic membership prospects) with regard to the EU and the WEU.[123] Upon developing a future free-trade zone attention should be given to synchronising the process. This applies to a future accession to the OECD as well. The three European CIS states' parallel membership of the WTO will be of decisive importance: an internationally binding solution could, in particular, be found for the problem of Ukrainian payment arrears towards Russia.[124]

NATO

Relations between NATO and Russia still need delicate treatment. Here, too, Russian policy is characterised by contradictions: although open opposition against the eastern enlargement of NATO continues to increase, there have been signs of compromise proposals. At the same time, Russia has proven to be a reliable and cooperative partner in implementing the Dayton accords in Bosnia. Jointly securing peace in the former Yugoslavia could break the path for new cooperation between Russia and NATO. This new perspective must be used for future military and political cooperation with Russia.

Long-drawn arguments over the eastern enlargement of NATO have shown that the following political principles must be upheld:
– Russia cannot be granted a right to veto NATO enlargement. It must accept the sovereign decision of the East Central European and the Baltic countries alike. Just as the West needs an active *Ostpolitik*, Russia has to develop an active *Westpolitik*.
– NATO enlargement must be closely coordinated and harmonised with the policy of the European Union (and the further development of the OSCE). In principle, the aim of parallel membership ought to be adhered to.

---

123 On the security problem of Ukraine cf. Alexandrova, Olga: Die Ukraine und die europäische Sicherheitsarchitektur, in: Aktuelle Analysen des BIOst No. 57, 1995.
124 Handelsblatt of 23 January 1996.

- Modelled on the 2+4 talks for Germany, nuclear weapons or foreign troops should not be stationed in the future Central and Eastern European member states in times of peace.
- A "first round" for NATO enlargement, consisting of a limited number of participants, must be based on a well-considered concept for those states which will at first be unable to join.[125] In principle, the option of future memberships and the introduction of associated partnerships must be given; modifying NATO's alliance character must also remain basically possible.

The key question of collective security is whether a "Strategic Security Pact" will be developed between NATO and Russia. Such an agreement, which would signal a historic breakthrough for both sides, would have to be complemented by parallel, but more limited, security treaties with Belarus and Ukraine. The agreements must become the central pillars of a future trilateral security partnership between the USA, Europe and the CIS. The basic principles of a first security document were adopted by the NATO Council of Ministers in Noordwijk in May 1995.[126] However, to date the suggestions have merely aimed at passing a declaration of principle or a charter. The objective should be a binding international treaty, based on the principles of the OSCE and a renunciation-of-violence declaration. The following core issues seem to be particularly recommendable:

- the formation of a permanent organ for consultation between NATO and Russia. It should be established within the framework of the North Atlantic Council and the other NATO committees (DPC, NPG). A smaller group ought to be founded in addition to the "16+1" or "17 round".[127]
- the speedy establishment of permanent bilateral missions between NATO and Russia in Moscow and Brussels. These missions should serve to maintain regular contacts and be important channels for in-

---

125 For first proposals cf. Asmus, Ronald D. and Larrabee, F. Stephen: NATO and the Have-Nots, Reassurance After Enlargement, in: Foreign Affairs, Vol. 75, No. 6, November/December 1996, pp. 13–20.

126 Presse- und Informationsamt der Bundesregierung (ed.): Kommuniqué der Ministertagung des Nordatlantikrats, in: Bulletin No. 48, 1995, p. 425.

127 This could be modelled on the "3+1 group" and comprise the USA, one representative from Germany, Great Britain or France, and - in rotation - one representative of the smaller NATO states.

tensive public relations efforts. In Russia, the distorted image of NATO, still dating back to Soviet times, must urgently be corrected.
- the further development of the cooperation and consultation mechanisms envisaged in the Partnership for Peace (PFP). The operative potential cooperation established in the PfP is to be detached from the debate on enlargement and developed separately. The above-mentioned bilateral consultation mechanism should be complemented for Russia within the scope of the "Individual Partnership Programme (IPP)".
- the further development of military cooperation, based on the first experiences gained in the joint IFOR and SFOR operations.
- Beyond military questions, the strategic partnership between NATO and Russia should be further developed with a view to a new agenda of more widely defined common security risks: apart from disarmament and cooperation in arms production, conflict prevention, environmental protection and humanitarian aid should be given more importance.

Institutionalisation of the Bosnia contact group

The success of the Bosnia contact group has shown that, despite conflicting interests, Europe, the USA and Russia can find constructive methods to settle conflicts. This lesson, and the practical experience gained in the IFOR and SFOR operations, should be further developed and institutionalised. The contact group, as a small group outside the NATO context, offers an interesting forum for dialogue, notably with Russia. It could accompany and prepare the discussion of all above-mentioned subjects. In future, however, Central and Eastern Europe as well as Ukraine must be firmly included. For that purpose, membership could be extended as follows: besides Russia, the USA, Germany, France and Great Britain, Ukraine should join as permanent member. Furthermore, the smaller western states and the CEE states each ought to take part with one (rotating) representative.

Consolidation of the OSCE

Ultimately, strengthening the OSCE is in the interest of both Moscow and the West. The OSCE, as the only European organisation in which Russia, the CIS states and the USA are represented, offers the best enlarged framework for a trilateral security partnership. Russia's suggestions for strengthening the OSCE, in particular for establishing a "European Security Council", should be taken up and further developed. Here the contact group could also serve as starting point; in specific cases, representatives of relevant parties to the conflict should be consulted.

The West and the other CIS member states

As regards the future of the post-Soviet space, the western community must clearly define its aims and interests. It is an illusion to believe that the CIS could become a supranational integration community, similar to the EU. Neither is it wise in principle to reject all attempts made at integration on the territory of the former USSR. Close cooperation and integration of individual CIS states is in the West's long-term interest, if they are based on free-will and democratic decisions: not only would Russia be integrated, but the whole Euro-Asian space would be stabilised. Supranational integration would also help to settle the numerous national-ethnic conflicts and bridge the gap threatening to separate the six Muslim-oriented CIS states from Europe.

Since, in the long term, the CIS will hardly survive as an integration community, the West should not upgrade it by institutional contacts. Instead, political stabilisation and national independence of the individual CIS members ought to be specifically promoted. Beyond its future eastern border zones, the EU should maintain the intensive political dialogue provided in all partnership agreements. It should also support the development of democratic and constitutional structures in the other CIS member states. While reinforcing the political stability of individual regional powers (Azerbaijan, Georgia), new beginnings of regional cooperation (Caucasus, Central Asia) ought to be specifically supported.

Russian efforts to enforce an old-style reintegration by means of military and security policy must be opposed by a western interest in a "new" supranational integration community. Within the scope of the proposed trilateral dialogue, the West should stress that all integration steps – on CIS or regional level – must follow the UN and CSCE principles. An agreement on the main outlines of a common CIS policy within the framework of an all-European security agenda should be the long-term aim. In promoting an adequate integration model, the focus must not be placed solely on the EU. Other regional alliances, like e. g. NAFTA, are also to be examined so as to find out whether they could offer a more suitable alternative to the CIS.[128]

Particular attention is to be paid to the fourth future European CIS neighbour, Moldavia. The little southern republic has made more progress in its democratic stabilisation and economic consolidation than could be expected: the way in which autonomy for the Gagauz minority was regulated is considered a model for similar cases.[129] Even though the question of direct neighbourhood will probably not be raised in a first enlargement round of NATO or the EU, two reasons force the West to concentrate on this CIS republic, as well: the presence of the 14th Russian Army in a future EU neighbour state, and the unsolved problem of a possible reunification with the future EU partner, Romania. The EU partnership agreement has already offered Moldavia, as fourth CIS state, the prospects of a free-trade area. In the same way, the principle of equality with Russia, Belarus and Ukraine ought to be transferred increasingly to all multilateral forums (NATO, NACC, OSCE, IMF, EBRD). The problem of Russian troops in Transdniestr must, in particular, be solved on the international level; mainly the OSCE, which has been active in a long-term mission in Moldavia since 1992, but also the UN or the WEU, ought to be considered as relevant actors.

Moreover, Moldavia is a good example for the difficult attempt at pursuing a neutral "seesaw policy" between western structures and the CIS, which other CIS countries, less willing to integrate, might also consider. A new institutionalised system of "non-aligned states" must, therefore,

---

128 Cf. Zagorskij Andrej: Was für eine GUS erfüllt ihren Zweck?, in: Außenpolitik No. 3, 1995, pp. 263–270.
129 Gabanyi, Anneli Ute: Moldawien im Spannungsfeld zwischen Rußland, Rumänien und der Ukraine, in: Berichte des BIOst, No. 16, 1996.

be considered within the framework of a future trilateral partnership. For a long time, the union of "non-aligned countries", which had developed in the Cold War period under the auspices of Yugoslavia, contributed to neutralising the East-West conflict. For Ukraine, but also for Moldavia and Azerbaijan, the safest strategy for the future might lie in a "free" alliance (possibly operating under the shelter of the OSCE), which Moscow would have to respect.

Conflict prevention and settlement in the former Soviet Union constitute one of the greatest challenges to the future trilateral partnership. For the West, long-term active involvement on the territory of the CIS is at stake. Europe and the United States should, in principle, face up to their basic joint responsibility and try to coordinate their efforts. With the aim of concluding a trilateral agreement, they ought to develop a regional concept to secure peace in the CIS, which should be based on the following conditions:

1. Russia must realise its interest in a cooperative conflict settlement in the CIS. As soon as Moscow wants to reinforce the OSCE as security organisation, it cannot be interested in undermining the role of the OSCE in the CIS area.

2. The objective of the western CIS policy is not to eliminate, but to diversify and control Russian influence. For this purpose, the OSCE principles which could not be adopted in Budapest in 1994 must be taken up anew and further developed – perhaps on a trilateral level (international control of Russian peace-keeping forces, multinationality of missions, strengthened role of the OSCE).[130]

3. The exploitation of energy deposits in the Caspian Sea is a dangerous problem, which must be solved on the international level, so as to be binding for all sides and secure stability.

4. The long-term missions of the OSCE in the CIS (Georgia, Moldavia, Ukraine, Tajikistan as well as the "supportive mission" in Chechnya, and mainly the "Minsk Group" dealing with the conflict in Nagorno-Karabakh) are the starting-point for a permanent and internationally guaranteed conflict management within the CIS. In order to bring the mis-

---

130 Schneider, Heinrich: Das Budapester Überprüfungstreffen und der Budapester Gipfel, in: OSZE-Jahrbuch 1995, Baden-Baden 1995, pp. 420–422.

sions to a successful conclusion, the political will of the West will be as decisive as cooperative behaviour on Russia's side. The memorandum on the settlement of the South-Ossetian conflict, signed in Moscow in May 1996, could be an important starting point.[131]

5. Modelled on the OSCE missions in Estonia, Latvia and Ukraine, additional OSCE long-term missions for the settlement of Russian minority questions should be established in all CIS states concerned.

6. In addition, with a view to the long-term potential conflicts in Central Asia, the presence of the OSCE must be decisively reinforced there. The branch of the Office for Democratic Institutions and Human Rights in Tashkent can serve as first starting point.

Moreover, the OSCE must prepare itself for active peace-keeping operations in the CIS. The future "European Security Council" could receive a key role. Meanwhile, the "Minsk Group" has become a first model; following the pattern of the contact group, it deals with the most demanding OSCE project in the CIS, i.e. pacifying the conflict between Armenia and Azerbaijan over the enclave of Nagorno-Karabakh.[132] Since the Budapest CSCE summit in December 1994, at which the decision to send an OSCE peace-keeping force was taken, preparations have made no progress beyond the planning stage. Even so, the planned operation of a peace-keeping force, comprising up to 5 000 troops, is the most important international test case to establish peace in the post-Soviet area. With a view to common Russian, American and European long-term interests in safeguarding pipeline routes throughout the region, securing peace in Nagorno-Karabakh could become the catalyst of a joint CIS conflict management on the trilateral level.

---

131 Cf. Moskovskye Novosti issues of 19–26 May 1996. Even according to Russian judgement, the OSCE was involved in this memorandum to a great extent. Implementing the memorandum would not only help to settle the conflict in Abkhasia, but also decisively strengthen the OSCE's role as mediator all over the CIS territory and even in Chechnya.
132 Ganser, Helmut W.: Die Bemühungen der OSZE um die Beilegung des Konfliktes um Berg-Karabach, in: OSZE Jahrbuch 1995, op. cit., pp. 187ff.

Programme for nuclear and ecological redevelopment

It is equally a European task to cope with the nuclear and ecological heritage of the Soviet Union. Problems of nuclear proliferation, nuclear traffic and "loose nukes" must not remain the exclusive domain of Russian-American cooperation; instead, they must be made a core issue within a future trilateral partnership between the USA, Europe and Russia. There is still an enormous number of related problems, and costs will rise in order to solve them. With a view to the extent of the imminent dangers, concerted action of the USA and all OECD states is required. In order to limit the damage, an extensive nuclear and ecological redevelopment programme should be developed for those CIS states which have been hardest hit.

In addition to the promised US financial aid, European funds must be made available to Kazakhstan in order to close down and seal the nuclear test area and fight against long-term damage to the population's health. Kazakhstan as the largest Central Asian state and second most important integration partner of Russia, assumes a key role in Eurasia.

As a new nation state, Belarus remains a highly fragile construction. The West has, therefore, a vital interest in supporting Minsk more strongly in fighting against the effects of Chernobyl. Similar to Kazakhstan, Belarus should also be rewarded for successfully completing its programme of de-nuclearisation. The most difficult problem is Ukraine. In December 1995 a memorandum was signed between the G 7, the European Commission and the Ukrainian government, proposing a compensation programme for closing down the Chernobyl reactor, but to date it has not yet become binding. The disputed questions on financing must finally be settled.[133] An agreement with a binding schedule must be concluded, on which the closing down of other RBMK reactors should be modelled. As soon as a final solution will have been agreed on, the suggestion of establishing an "International Chernobyl Fund" should be taken up, which was made by the "Alliance" consortium, winner of the EU call for tenders for a feasibility study in 1995.[134] Establishing an in-

---

[133] On the latest frictions between the G 7 countries and the EBRD on Ukraine's energy programme cf. "Tschernobyl als Faustpfand" in: Frankfurter Allgemeine Zeitung of 10 February 1997.
[134] Hahn, Dorothea: Eine Christo-Lösung für Tschernobyl, die tageszeitung of 14 March 1996.

ternational research centre to deal with the experiences gained from the worst catastrophe in the civil use of nuclear power would also be in the interest of all G 7 states. In principle, western programmes must, in future, concentrate on more measures to save energy: on estimate, all CIS states would be capable of saving energy up to 40 to 50 percent of the current power consumption.[135]

A special framework for the problems related to scrapping Russian or ex-Soviet nuclear weapons should be created within the scope of the future consultation mechanisms between NATO and Russia (and the Russian partnership programme of "PfP" respectively). The International Atomic Energy Agency (IAEA) ought to be more deeply involved here. Western assistance has, so far, concentrated on increasing the safety of nuclear transports; in future the focus must be placed on safe storage places and the disposal of nuclear arms material. Political meetings, such as the "Nuclear Summit" of the G 7, should, moreover, be made a regular institution. Such meetings serve to coordinate the actors and put public pressure on the states concerned, such as Russia or Ukraine. In addition, the complex risks of the nuclear heritage of the USSR is made known to an international public. Before a next nuclear summit, Russia must be induced to take another three important steps:

– It must implement the Russian-American paper of May 1995 on the "transparency and irreversibility of the process of reducing nuclear weapons". Until now, Russia has not met the agreement, which provides for regular exchanges of detailed data and mutual inspections of plants;
– it is to sign the 1993 London Convention prohibiting the disposal of radioactive waste into the sea; and
– it must join the Vienna Convention on compensation for damage caused by nuclear accidents.

American experts have made several serious suggestions to fight trafficking and proliferation of uncontrolled nuclear material. The focus is placed on an extensive data exchange and so-called "buyback bargains", following the example of Kazakhstan.[136] Europeans must realise that

---

135 Breyer, Hiltrud: Tschernobyl und die Europäische Union, in: BBU infodienst No. 6/1, 1996, p. 15.
136 Cf. Allison, Graham T.: Avoiding Nuclear Anarchy, in: International Security No. 12, 1996, pp. 146ff.

this problem is a first-rate security risk and make themselves heard in the trilateral dialogue with the USA and Russia. The non-nuclear residual damage in the CIS states cannot be further ignored either. Environmental cooperation must become the centre of cooperation with the CIS, but also of transnational initiatives with the countries of Central and Eastern Europe. Apart from financial means (also for more extensive environmental monitoring), a far-reaching transfer of training and know-how is required from the West. On the official level, programmes for a more effective use of energy should be developed; they ought to be complemented by public information campaigns. In almost all CIS states, the populations are insufficiently informed about how to protect themselves against ecological risks.

V. Overcoming the new borders

The eastern enlargement of the EU and NATO alike will fundamentally change the European order. In the east, Euro-Atlantic structures will move forward to the territories of Belarus and Ukraine; a common frontier with the CIS members Russia, Belarus and Ukraine will develop from the Barents Sea to the Black Sea. When the Baltic states enter the EU, part of the Russian territory – the region around Kaliningrad – will become an enclave within the EU. In the foreseeable future, the European Union will directly border the Balkan countries, as Slovenia, Romania and Bulgaria have a firm option for accession.

Until now, the European Union has not fully discussed the question of the strategic consequences of eastern enlargement. The problems of the future EU border zones in the east and southeast have, however, already become manifest. A Union of 27 would be directly concerned by conflicts in these regions. Political instability, social disturbances and mass emigration in the future neighbour states in the Balkans and the CIS would at once have their effects on security and stability in the EU. The Union needs accountable and reliable partners at its borders. In addition to its strategies for enlargement, peace and partnership, the EU must early on work out a concept for all-European neighbourhood, which can guarantee security and stability for Europe as a whole in the medium term.

Such an all-European concept aims at balancing the differences in stability and prosperity existing alongside the future borders in the east and southeast of Europe. This can only be obtained by speedily building up stable democratic and market economy systems in the future neighbour states. At the same time, as early as today constructive and cooperative relations between the Union and its future neighbours must be developed. In order to achieve both these aims, forms of transnational cooperation must be supported soon and systematically. Existing and new initiatives comprising the EU, Central and Eastern Europe, the Balkans and the CIS are to be dealt with. These initiatives must be further developed on the supranational, national and subnational level alike.

1. Strengthening the OSCE and the Council of Europe

Strengthening the OSCE and the Council of Europe should play a central role on the multilateral level. Both these organisations are all-European institutions and comprise states from all three Eastern European territories; therefore they are particularly important for the future development of the European continent.

Contents and institution of the OSCE must, in consequence, be revaluated. In terms of contents, work on the "Stability Pact in Europe" is to be continued. The treaty, which was concluded in March 1995, constitutes a great success of preventive diplomacy in Europe. By concluding the basic treaty between Hungary and Slovakia, the dangers of the Slovak-Hungarian minority conflict could be diminished. Moreover, the open questions about the border between Lithuania and Belarus were answered by adding a corresponding contract to the Stability Pact.[137] Three more steps should be made as soon as possible:
– In order to defuse the smouldering border conflicts in the Baltic area, border treaties between Estonia and Russia as well as between Latvia and Russia ought to be concluded as quickly as possible.
– To date, the talks within the scope of the Stability Pact have mainly dealt with minority and border questions; in future they should also include fields such as arms control or economic cooperation. More-

---

137 Cf. Agence Europe of 22 March 1995.

over negotiations, which have until now been limited to Central and Eastern Europe and the CIS, are to be extended to the southern Balkans.
– The financial aid granted by the EU to support the Stability Pact ought to be increased selectively. Via PHARE the Union has made approximately ECU 260 m available to support regional, border-crossing co-operation and to strengthen democratic structures in Central and Eastern Europe. Measured against more than 100 individual projects which were launched within the framework of the Stability Pact the financial aid granted by the EU has been rather modest.[138]

In addition, the OSCE must be further developed institutionally so as to become more effective. An enlarged Union would become the direct neighbour of the unsettled conflicts in the Balkans and the CIS. Extensive strengthening of the OSCE is, therefore, not only in the interest of Russia; it should be the target of all states of a future EU of 27:[139]

– All OSCE institutions should be assembled in Vienna, where the permanent secretariat and the Centre for Conflict Prevention have their headquarters. This would limit frictional losses in the daily work which might evolve from the institutions' being distributed over several European cities (Warsaw, Prague, Geneva, The Hague, Copenhagen). Furthermore, financial and personal contributions of the OSCE members will have to be increased if the OSCE is to fulfil higher operative demands in the future.

– In order to become less dependent on the respective OSCE presidency, the secretary-general's mandate should be extended. Whether to grant the office of the secretary-general early warning authority of its own, or the opportunities to intervene and mediate in order to prevent conflicts, ought to be taken into consideration. In addition, a strong OSCE secretariat-general would have to be established. This would be important to ensure the OSCE's functioning, in particular in the transition period until a European Security Council is founded.

---

138 Cf. Hausmann, Hartmut: Stabilitätspakt für Europa, Europäische Zeitung No. 4, 1995.
139 On some of the following considerations cf. Lutz, Dieter S.: Die OSZE im Übergang der Sicherheitsarchitektur des Zwanzigsten Jahrhunderts zum Sicherheitsmodell des Einundzwanzigsten Jahrhunderts, in: Institut für Friedensforschung und Sicherheitspolitik an der Universität Hamburg (ed.): OSZE-Jahrbuch 1995, Baden-Baden 1995, pp. 63–96, and Hennig, Ortwin: Die KSZE/OSZE aus deutscher Sicht - Kein Wechsel der Unterstützung, in: ibd., pp. 121–135.

- In the medium term, the OSCE is to be based on the principles of international law. To transform the OSCE into the central directive authority to settle national and international conflicts all over Europe, binding norms and methods for preventing and settling conflicts as well as possible sanctions must be laid down.
- The principle of unanimity (or the "consensus minus one" rule) in the OSCE ought to be given up in favour of an extension of the principle of majority vote. In future, consensus should be exclusively required for basic rulings whereas all other questions would be decided by a qualified majority. Equality of all member countries would thus, in principle, be maintained while at the same time the OSCE's capacity to make decisions and its functioning would be improved decisively.

Whereas the OSCE as an instrument of preventive diplomacy could take over monitoring and mediating functions, the Council of Europe could concentrate on further developing the European protective norms of human and minority rights. The OSCE's role would then mainly be to manage ethnic problems. The Council of Europe, by contrast, would control the quality. All activities of the Council of Europe would aim at establishing a European legal territory which guarantees legal norms of western democracies all over Europe.

In its present state, the Council of Europe is not equal to this task. In recent years there have been several cases of new entries in which the basic prerequisite, i.e. the fulfilment of European norms, was dodged (Slovakia, Albania, Russia). Even Turkey, which has already been a member for a long time, openly violates human rights standards. The Council of Europe needs structural reforms in order to be strengthened for its future tasks. This will be the only way to ensure that the Council of Europe remains able to act and decide despite its increasing number of members.[140]

Introducing qualified majority vote decisions in the Committee of

---

140 The suggestions are partly based on Antretter, Robert: Aus den Lehren der Vergangenheit die politische Zukunft des Europarats gestalten, in: Antretter, Robert (ed.): Quo vadis Europarat?, Bonn 1995, pp. 7–11; Fischer, Leni: Ausuferung droht: Straffung der parlamentarischen Arbeit unverzichtbar, in: ibd., pp. 12–15; and Klebes, Heinrich: Menschenrechte, Minderheitenschutz: Markenzeichen des Europarats, in: ibd., pp. 16–21.

Ministers is long overdue; until now, it has been restricted to a few cases only. At the same time, parliamentary structures of the Council of Europe must be streamlined (cutting down the number of representatives, accelerating work in the committees etc.).

Further development of the Framework Convention for the Protection of National Minorities (1995) is indispensable. Regulations laid down in the convention are still rather indistinctly formulated. The control mechanism (periodical reports by the parties to the contract to the Committee of Ministers) is noncommittal. The Convention on Human Rights as well as the Convention on Minorities ought to be equipped with a catalogue providing concrete sanctions in case of disregard. Moreover, the Additional Protocol of the European Convention on Human Rights, which deals with the cultural rights of minorities, must be finished and ratified as soon as possible.

More than before, the Council's programmes which aim at building up civil societies in Eastern Europe (e. g. "Demosthenes" and "Lode") should be supported. Campaigns against xenophobia, antisemitism and intolerance; courses on the freedom of the press and democracy on the local level; and projects for the integration of minority groups must, in particular, be intensified; more meeting centres for young people from various Eastern European countries are to be installed.

2. Developing regional cooperation

Another element within the concept of all-European neighbourhood is the skilful development of regional cooperation. In this context, the EU must first of all strengthen regional initiatives which already exist. The focus should be placed on forms of cooperation which go beyond possible future divides. Defining common regional interests should play a major role in the process of solving problems.

The following regional initiatives are to be supported: the Central European Free-Trade Area (CEFTA), the Baltic Sea Council, the Central European Initiative and the Black Sea Cooperation and the Southeast

European Cooperative Initiative.[141] Apart from CEFTA they comprise all states of the EU, Central and Eastern Europe, and also of the Balkans and the CIS. Consolidating these regional associations could result in the Balkans and the CIS being more closely tied to the process of European integration. These forms of regional cooperation should be made use of in the policy pursued with regard to the future neighbours:

- As early as today, CEFTA should prepare the integration of additional Balkan and CIS states (mainly Croatia and Ukraine) and, early on, start first negotiations. In the meantime, CEFTA and future accession countries ought to reduce mutual customs tariffs and quotas; tax and trade laws would have to be adjusted to each other. In addition, continuously liberalising the sectors of agriculture, industry, services and capital would help to develop CEFTA further in terms of contents.
- The Baltic Sea Council consists of four EU member states (Germany, Denmark, Finland and Sweden), four CEE states (Poland, Estonia, Latvia, Lithuania), Norway and Russia. There are still grave, unsolved problems in trade and traffic between the countries bordering on the Baltic Sea. They are mainly caused by harassing customs procedures on the main route from Germany via Poland into the Baltic states and Russia (Via Baltica). In order to accelerate the economic development in the whole Baltic region, new checkpoints and an homogeneous and more effective border control system in the member states of the Baltic Council are required. Training programmes and language courses for border officials could, on both sides, help to facilitate border controls.
- To date, apart from the EU member states Italy and Austria, five CEE states (Poland, the Czech Republic, Slovakia, Slovenia and Hungary), six Balkan countries (Albania, Bosnia-Herzegovina, Bulgaria, Croatia, Macedonia and Romania) as well as three CIS states (Moldavia, Ukraine and Belarus) are represented in the Central European Initiative (CEI). To be joined by the Federal Republic of Yugoslavia should be the major objective of the CEI. Within its framework, important routes (as, for example, the route Jesenice-Ljubljana-Zagreb-

---

141 For information about these regional initiatives cf. Meier, Christian: Wirtschaftsbeziehungen zwischen den Staaten Osteuropas: Regionale Kooperation auf dem Prüfstand, in: Berichte des BIOst No. 36, 1995.

Belgrade, Niš-Skopje or Vienna-Budapest-Novi Sad-Belgrade) ought to be constructed; waterways (e. g. Danube and Save) should be further developed; energy and telecommunications networks must be modernised. The CEI needs financial incentives to make progress independently; the EU should therefore make funds available via PHARE so as to cofinance projects organised by the CEI. The so-called "human dimension" of the CEI must also be further advanced. The document on the protection of minorities, which was worked out in 1994, is a good starting point.

− The Black Sea Cooperation (BSC) comprises a very diversified group of Eastern European regional states: Greece as EU member state; Turkey; two CEE states (Romania, Bulgaria); Albania, representing the Balkans; as well as six CIS states (Armenia, Azerbaijan, Georgia, Moldavia, Russia, Ukraine). In order to settle national and international conflicts, the BSC must be institutionalised to a higher degree. Until now there have been only two working organs: the Council of Foreign Ministers, which meets once a year, and a parliamentary assembly. Permanent BSC headquarters, a managing secretariat and working groups should also be established; they would deal with settling conflicts and coordinate cooperation among members on the political level. In order to promote economic development in the Black Sea region, adequate preconditions for project-oriented economic cooperation are to be created. These would have to be supported by the EU giving technical assistance and know-how. The EU could also get involved in the development of the Bank for Development and Investment which was founded within the framework of the BSC. The long-term objective beyond these initiatives is to establish a free-trade area within the Black Sea region.

− The members of the Southeast European Cooperative Initiative (SECI) are also very heterogeneous: one EU member state (Greece); Turkey; four CEE states (Bulgaria, Hungary, Romania, Slovenia); four Balkan states (Albania, Bosnia-Herzegovina, Croatia, Former Yugoslav Republic of Macedonia); as well as the CIS state Moldavia. In order to promote regional economic growth, the EU should support infrastructure development (transportation, roads, the Danube) as well as trade facilitation (border crossings, transporting goods, customs procedures) within SECI. In this context the EU is to cooperate closely with the (planned) Business Advisory Committee of SECI, which will act as a link to the business community.

Since number and size of the regional initiatives in Eastern Europe are constantly rising, the EU should carefully direct and coordinate all their activities to avoid mutual interference. Ultimately, intensified cooperation and networking activities in the newly developing Eastern European regions cannot be limited to regional initiatives. Another prerequisite is the normalisation and deepening of political relations on the bilateral level. The Central and Eastern European states play a key role. After their integration into the EU they will have an important bridging function at the borders between the EU and the countries of the Balkans and the CIS. To date, almost all CEE states have, in political and economic terms, concentrated too much on a consistent westward orientation. In an enlarged EU, however, security and stability will be based on the future EU member states developing a policy of good-neighbourly relations at their eastern and southeastern borders. For this purpose, the foreign policy of the CEE states requires a new orientation.

For the Central and Eastern European states this mainly means to normalise the historically burdened relations with Russia, but also with Ukraine. In order to increase effectiveness, the bilateral cooperation on the level of governments and parliaments as well as regional cooperation must be institutionalised, increasingly integrating non-government organisations as well. The CEE states could here return to their experience gained in the "structured dialogue" with the EU. Military cooperation between Central and Eastern Europe and the neighbour states in the Balkans and the CIS must also be consolidated. Poland's cooperation with Ukraine could work as a model; apart from planning cooperation between military districts close to the border and collaboration in questions of armament technology, both states intend to muster joint forces for UN peace-keeping missions.[142] In the long run, however, getting rid of traditional concepts of the enemy, which have, mainly in the case of Russia, determined a great deal of bilateral relations until today, will be decisive. The difficult task of dealing with the common history must be tackled.

---

142 Cf. Frankfurter Allgemeine Zeitung of 27 June 1996.

Modelled on the normalisation of German-Polish relations, which started in the early 1970s, establishing common historian and textbook commissions could often be a first step to assess the "blanks".

3. Promoting cooperation between border regions

The development of the European Union has shown that the Western European states have grown together, in particular at their borders. Cross-border cooperation between regions and communities has become an integral part of European unification. It has bridged gaps and created human relations across all borders. All sides benefit from advantages of specialisation so that regional cooperation constitutes an important factor for mutual economic development. This experience is to be integrated into the EU's present policy towards Eastern Europe in order to pass the danger point of future divides.

The most promising form of supporting cooperation between border regions is to create and develop so-called "Euro-regions". Several of these "Euro-regions" between the EU member states and their Central and Eastern European neighbours have already come into being and obtained pioneer status.[143] At present there are, however, only two initiatives between Central and Eastern Europe and the CIS along the future Eastern border of the EU:

- The Euro-region Carpathia was created in 1993 and comprises border districts of Poland, Hungary, Slovakia and Ukraine. Since then, several joint committees have been formed; exhibitions, economic forums and cultural events have been organised; the universities have founded an association.
- The Euro-region Bug was established in 1995 by Polish and Ukrainian border districts. The first working groups were formed in April 1996. To date, only ecological projects have been agreed on.

---

143 Cf. e.g. the Euro-regions Bavarian Forest/Bohemian Forest, Egrensis, Elbe/Labe, Oder-Neisse, Spree-Neisse-Bober or Pomerania.

The further development of both initiatives is faced by numerous problems. Some governments, foremost among them the Slovak government, critically oppose the projects. Reasons can be found in bilateral conflicts (such as Slovak-Hungarian relations) and in the fear of transferring decision-making competences from the centre to the regions. The uncertain situation of local self-administration as well as differences in the administrative structures of the participating states represent another problem. Moreover, with a view to the problems created by transformation, funds available to the participating states are extremely meagre. There are also difficulties due to different customs, foreign currency and tax provisions. The regions concerned basically lack experience in the field of institutionalising transnational cooperation.

Given the major importance of such projects, a central information and advisory bureau for Euro-regions ought to be created by the EU. It could be modelled on the information office established for the implementation of the White Paper on the preparation for the internal market. Such an office would have the following tasks:

- It should advise the participating states in legal and technical issues. The Union has gained extensive experience in dealing with its existing Euro-regions, which is to be made available to the Eastern European regions without reservations.
- In addition, it would coordinate PHARE and TACIS aid programmes for Central and Eastern Europe and the CIS in a better way. Both EU programmes need to be more closely coordinated in order to intensify transnational cooperation.

Individual Eastern European governments which hinder the creation of Euro-regions in their borderland are to be admonished by the EU to cooperate actively. It is important to stress that good will and capacity with regard to regional cooperation will be significant criteria when it comes to assessing the future member states' integration capacity into the EU.

The region of Kaliningrad, which belongs to Russia, should immediately become a geographical focal point of regional cooperation.[144] After the EU integration of Poland and Lithuania, the region would become a

---

144 For information on Kaliningrad cf. Swerew, Iurij M.: Rußlands Gebiet Kaliningrad im neuen geopolitischen Koordinatenfeld, in: Berichte des BIOst No. 6, 1996.

Russian enclave within the Union. Therefore stabilising the region of Kaliningrad is not only in the interest of Russia, but also of the Union and the associated states of Central and Eastern Europe. The previous development of Kaliningrad indicates another direction. Due to the uncertain legal situation, insufficient infrastructure and the large Russian military presence, western investment in the Kaliningrad region remains low. The traditional economic ties with Lithuania have been cut. Trade with Poland stagnates on the lowest level. New dynamism requires new initiatives:

- founding the Euro-region Nyemen – already planned (since 1995) –, which is to comprise the Lithuanian, Polish and Belarussian border communities and parts of the Kaliningrad region;
- extending TACIS aids to the Kaliningrad region;
- counselling Russia and the other states concerned on the development of safe legal principles for the Kaliningrad region. Transit from Kaliningrad via Lithuania and Poland to Russia must be regulated in a binding form. The economic programmes should aim at establishing a free-trade zone on the Kaliningrad territory, in which no customs would be due and considerable investment and tax incentives would be granted to foreign investors.
- integrating the Kaliningrad region into projects of the Baltic Sea Council. Infrastructure projects are preferably to be supported: the planned extension of the harbour, the airport and the telecommunications system as well as the railway lines Kaliningrad-Kaunas-Vilnius-Minsk and Berlin-Szczecin-Gdansk-Kaliningrad.
- negotiating a reduction of forces in Kaliningrad within the framework of the cooperation between NATO and Russia. The EU should cover part of the costs for the withdrawal of the Russian soldiers and grant structural aid to the region, thus to create a demilitarised zone around Kaliningrad.

4. Networking Europe

The success of transnational initiatives also depends on an all-European network. Transeuropean Networks (TEN) are of major importance in this context. Roads and railway lines planned by the EU could decisively stimulate the trade with the regions newly opened, thus assuming fundamental importance for the development of economic prosperity all over Europe. The energy and communications networks planned within the scope of TEN have a similar rank. The conceptual development of Transeuropean Networks must therefore not remain limited to the enlarged EU. On the contrary, it is necessary early on to include the countries of the CIS and the Balkans into the planning and development phases of Transeuropean Networks.

Projects of prime importance are, for example, the development of the main roads from Lubeck via Szczecin, Gdansk, Kaliningrad and Riga to St Petersburg (Via Hanseatica) or from Berlin via Warsaw and Minsk to Moscow. Within the field of energy, further improvement of oil and gas pipelines from Russia to the EU is as urgent as the planned integrated electricity system "Baltic Ring" (which is to comprise the Baltic states, Denmark, Sweden, Finland, Germany, Poland, Russia and Belarus).[145]

The EU cannot be the only party to generate Transeuropean Networks. However, the Union can take over an important function as catalyst and coordinator of the various projects. It should promote contacts between investors and users, but also introduce common standards, thus contributing to individual units of the future Transeuropean Networks becoming compatible so as to be connected. In addition, the EU can create incentives for private investors by way of pilot projects, feasibility studies, guarantees or subsidised interest rates.

Another initiative for an all-European network is the European Energy Charter, founded by the EU in 1991. Its aim is to build up a European energy market. Until now, the necessary framework conditions to offer western enterprises incentives for investment into the Eastern Eu-

---

[145] Cf. Objectives, Modalities and Priority Projects for the Transeuropean Networks in the Field of Energy, Agence Europe of 5 June 1996.

ropean energy sector have not been established. Entering into new negotiations is therefore required in order to improve the situation in the field of investment protection, energy trade, transit of energy products, but also in environmental protection.

Ultimately, Europe cannot be merely technically connected. A closer interweaving of different initiatives on the political level will be decisive for the future. Better coordination of the complete European *Ostpolitik* is indispensable for this purpose. In terms of concepts, the EU, but also NATO, must coordinate their association strategies towards the states of Central and Eastern Europe with their policies towards the Balkans and the CIS. At present cooperation, as a rule, takes place either with the Central and Eastern European countries or with the countries of the Balkans or the CIS respectively; cooperation does not yet exist across these borders. In future, this strategic deficit must be eliminated. New transnational paradigms for cooperation, which include the countries of all three regions, should be worked out.

The so-called "Weimar Triangle" could serve as a model. Within the scope of this initiative, there has been active cooperation between France, Germany and Poland since 1991. Annual meetings on the ministerial and parliamentary level take place between these three states, in the course of which common positions are formulated and initiatives are adopted. Moreover there are trilateral military manœuvres as well as meetings of young people and cultural activities. The Ukrainian President Kuchma suggested to integrate Ukraine into the trilateral cooperation between Paris, Bonn and Warsaw. If the three states approved an enlargement into a "quadrangle", the "Weimar Initiative" could become a model for "unlimited cooperation" in a new, all-European community. Along the lines of this example, other EU states could form new triangles or quadrangles with representatives from Central and Eastern Europe and the CIS or the Balkans (as, for example, Finland with Estonia and Russia, Austria with Hungary and Croatia). This would contribute decisively to toning down possible differences in Europe.

The strategies for a new *Ostpolitik* here presented show the way into an all-European future: the strategy for enlargement opens up prospects for a EU from Sicily to the North Cape, and from the Atlantic to the river Bug. By organising multi-track integration on a high, but varied level, the concept of differentiated integration guarantees that a "EU of 27" (or more) member states remains efficient. In the southeast of Europe, the strategy for peace for the Balkans will help to defuse ethnic conflicts and bring about economic modernisation. It offers a clear integration perspective to all countries of the region, which can lead to full EU membership in the long term. The strategy for partnership with Russia and the CIS supports the stable political and economic development of the post-Soviet area. By an extensive process of deepening and institutionalising relations, it will, furthermore, enable Russia and the CIS to develop closer ties to Europe. In connection with the concept of all-European neighbourhood, which supports a speedy linkage of the three Eastern European territories, the new *Ostpolitik* will be the fundament of a European community without new divides.

Appendix

Tables

Tab. 1: State of the Association Agreements (AAg) between the EU and the Central and Eastern European states

Country	AAg signed on	AAg in force since	applied for membership in
Bulgaria	8 March 1993	1 February 1995	December 1995
Czech Republic	4 October 1993	1 February 1995	January 1996
Estonia	12 June 1995	–	November 1995
Hungary	16 December 1991	1 February 1994	April 1994
Latvia	12 June 1995	–	November 1995
Lithuania	12 June 1995	–	December 1995
Poland	16 December 1991	1 February 1994	April 1994
Romania	1 February 1993	1 February 1995	June 1995
Slovak Republic	4 October 1993	1 February 1995	June 1995
Slovenia	10 June 1996	–	June 1996

Source: Survey made by the Research Group on European Affairs, as of August 1996

Tab. 2: State of the Partnership and Cooperation Agreements (PCA) with Russia and the CIS

Country	PCA signed on	PCA in force since	interim agreement signed on	interim agreement in force since
Russia	24 June 1994	–	17 July 1995	1 February 1996
Ukraine	14 June 1994	–	1 June 1995	1 February 1996
Kazakhstan	23 January 1995	–	5 December 1995	–
Kirgizstan	9 February 1995	–	–	–
Moldavia	28 November 1994	–	2 October 1995	–
Belarus	6 March 1995	–	25 March 1995	–
Georgia	22 April 1996	–	–	–
Armenia	22 April 1996	–	–	–
Azerbaijan	22 April 1996	–	–	–
Uzbekistan	21 June 1996	–	–	–
Turkmenistan	Decision on exploratory talks 20 June 1995	–	–	–
Tajikistan	to date, no talks scheduled	–	–	–

Source: European Commission, as of May 1996

Tab. 3: State of the Partnership and Cooperation Agreements (PCA) with the Balkan states

Country	PCA signed on	PCA in force since
Albania	11 May 1992	1 January 1992
Bosnia-Herzegovina	–	–
Federal Republic of Yugoslavia	–	–
Croatia*	–	–
Macedonia	–	–

* On 11 April 1995, the Council of Foreign Ministers authorised the European Commission to enter into negotiations on concluding a Cooperation Agreement with Croatia. The EU stopped PHARE funds and talks on a Cooperation Agreement because of Croat violations of human rights in the summer of 1995.

Source: Survey of the Research Group on European Affairs, as of August 1996

Bibliography

Adler, Ulrich: Der Bedarf an Umweltschutzinvestitionen in Mittel- und Osteuropa, in: ifo Schnelldienst No. 29, 1995, pp. 10–21.

Alexandrova, Olga: Die Ukraine und die europäische Sicherheitsstruktur, in: Aktuelle Analysen des BIOst No. 57, 1995.

Alexandrova, Olga: Rußland und sein »nahes Ausland«, in: Berichte des BIOst No. 20, 1995.

Algieri, Franco et al.: Managing Security in Europe. The European Union and the Challenge of Enlargement, Gütersloh 1996.

Allison, Graham/Kaiser, Karl/Karaganov, Sergei: Hin zu einer neuen Gemeinschaft demokratischer Nationen, in: Internationale Politik No. 11 1996, pp. 1–6.

Altmann, Franz-Lothar et al.: Die zukünftige Erweiterung der Europäischen Union in Mittelosteuropa, in: Südosteuropa No. 5, 1995, pp. 235–258.

Antretter, Robert: Aus den Lehren der Vergangenheit die politische Zukunft des Europarats gestalten, in: Antretter, Robert (ed.): Quo vadis Europarat?, Bonn 1995, pp. 7–11.

Asmus, Ronald D./Larrabee, F. Stephen: NATO and the Have-Nots. Reassurance After Enlargement, in: Foreign Affairs, Vol. 75, No. 6, November/December 1996, pp. 13–20.

Asmus, Ronald D./Nurick, Robert C.: NATO enlargement and the Baltic states, in: Survival, Vol. 38, No. 2, Summer 1996, pp. 121–142.

Baldwin, Richard E.: Towards an Integrated Europe, London 1994.

Bertelsmann Foundation Publishers (eds.): Europe's Political Agenda for the Nineties, Gütersloh 1995.

Bishop, Gita: Optimism Wanes for a Prompt Cleanup, in: Transition 17. May 1996.

Blackwill, Robert D./Karaganov, Sergei A. (eds.): Damage Limitation or Crisis? Russia and the Outside World. CSIA Studies in International Security No. 5, Washington D. C. 1994.

Boeri, Tito/Scarpetta, Stefano: Regional Dimensions of Unemployment in Central and Eastern Europe and Social Barriers to Restructuring, EUI Working Paper ECO No. 95/17, Florence 1995.

Bonvicini, Gianni et al. (ed.): A Renewed Partnership for Europe. Tackling European Security Challenges by EU-NATO Interaction, Baden-Baden 1995/96.

Bricke, Dieter W.: Minderheiten im östlichen Mitteleuropa. Deutsche und europäische Optionen, Baden-Baden 1995.

Brunner, Georg: Nationality Problems and Minority Conflicts in Eastern Europe, Gütersloh 1996.

Bundesministerium für Wirtschaft (ed.): Wirtschaftslage und Reformprozesse in Mittel- und Osteuropa, Sammelband 1996, Berlin 1996.

Bundesministerium für Wirtschaft (ed.): Die Beratung Mittel- und Osteuropas beim Aufbau von Demokratie und sozialer Marktwirtschaft, Konzept und Beratungsprogramme der Bundesregierung, BMWi-Dokumentation No. 371, Bonn 1995.

Calic, Marie-Janine: Das Abkommen von Dayton. Chancen und Risiken des Friedensprozesses im ehemaligen Jugoslawien, SWP AP 2948, Ebenhausen March 1996.

Calic, Marie-Janine: Der Krieg in Bosnien-Hercegovina. Ursachen, Konfliktstrukturen, internationale Lösungsversuche, Frankfurt/M. 1995.

Calic, Marie-Janine (ed.): Friedenskonsolidierung im ehemaligen Jugoslawien: Sicherheitspolitische und zivile Aufgaben, SWP S 413, Ebenhausen 1996.

Centre for Economic Policy Research (CEPR): Flexible Integration: Towards a More Effective and Democratic Europe, London 1995.

Cichy, Ulrich E.: EU-Osterweiterung: Chancen, Risiken, Konvergenzkriterien, in: Wirtschaftsdienst No. 12, 1995, pp. 662–668.

Clement, Hermann: Integrations- und Desintegrationstendenzen in Osteuropa und der GUS, Working Paper No. 186, Osteuropa-Institut, Munich, December 1995.

Club von Florenz (ed.): Europa: Der unmögliche Status quo, Baden-Baden 1996.

Commission of the European Communities: Agricultural Situation and Prospects in the Central and Eastern European Countries – Summary Report, Working Document, Brussels 1995.

Commission of the European Communities: European Economy. Economic situation and economic reform in Central and Eastern Europe, Supplement C, Economic Reform Monitor No. 1 – May 1996, Luxembourg 1996.

Commission of the European Communities: Phare 1994 - Annual Report, COM (95) 366 final, Brussels 1995.

Commission of the European Communities: White Paper on the Preparation of the associated Countries of Central and Eastern Europe for Integration into the internal Market of the Union, COM (95) 163 final, Brussels 1995.

Commission of the European Communities: Progress report from the Commission to the European Council on the effects of enlargement by the associated countries of Central and Eastern Europe on the policies of the European Union, COM (95) 605, Brussels 1995.

Commission of the European Communities: Progress report from the Commission on the implementation of the European Community programme of policy and action in relation to the environment and sustainable development: / Towards sustainability /, COM (95) 624 final, Brussels 1996.

Czempiel, Ernst-Otto: Die Neuordnung Europas. Was leisten NATO und OSZE für die Kooperation mit Osteuropa und Rußland, in: Aus Politik und Zeitgeschichte 1–2/1997.

Dauderstädt, Michael: Osterweiterung der EU: Lösung ohne Problem, in: Wirtschaftsdienst No. 10, 1995, pp. 533–541.

Deubner, Christian: Deutsche Europapolitik: Von Maastricht nach Kerneuropa? Baden-Baden 1995.

Deubner, Christian/Janning, Josef: Zur Reform des Abstimmungsverfahrens im Rat der Europäischen Union: Überlegungen und Modellrechnungen, in: Integration No. 3, 1996, pp. 146–158.

Deutsch-Russischer Austausch et al.: Zur Situation der Menschen- und Bürgerrechte in Rußland, Materialien und Aufsätze, Berlin 1995.

Deutsche Bank Research (ed.): Osteuropa-Themen: Kroatien No. 165, 28 October 1996.

Deutsche Gesellschaft für Auswärtige Politik: Wandel der Systeme. Themenheft der Zeitschrift Internationale Politik No. 6, 1995.

Deutsche Gesellschaft für Auswärtige Politik: Restauration der Sowjetunion?, Themenheft der Zeitschrift Internationale Politik No. 11, 1995.

Deutsches Institut für Wirtschaftsforschung (ed.): Umweltschutz in Rußland: Rückläufige Emissionen, aber zunehmende Störfallrisiken, in: Wochenbericht No. 13, 1996, pp. 209–219.

Deutsches Institut für Wirtschaftsforschung (ed.): Reform der Agrarpolitik – weiterer Anpassungsbedarf, in: Wochenbericht No. 32, 1995, pp. 553–558.

Dewatripont, Mathias et al.: Flexible Integration: Towards a More Effective and Democratic Europe, London 1995.

European Bank for Reconstruction and Development : Transition report 1995, London 1995.

Fischer, Leni: Ausuferung droht: Straffung der parlamentarischen Arbeit unverzichtbar, in: Antretter, Robert (Hrsg.): Quo vadis Europarat?, Bonn 1995, pp. 12–15.

Franzmeyer, Fritz: Osterweiterung, Kerneuropa, Währungsunion – Zentrale Weichenstellungen in der Integrationspolitik, in: Integration No. 3, 1995, pp. 125–132.

Frankfurter Allgemeine Zeitung GmbH Informationsdienste (ed.): Osteuropa-Perspektiven – Jahrbuch 1995/96, Frankfurt/M. 1995.

Gabanyi, Anneli Ute: Moldova im Spannungsfeld zwischen Rußland, Rumänien und der Ukraine, in: Berichte des BIOst No. 16, 1996.

Gambles, Ian (ed.): A lasting peace in Cental Europe? The expansion of the European security-community, Chaillot Paper 20, Paris 1995.

Geißler, Frank: Transformation und Kooperation. Die ostmitteleuropäischen Systemumbrüche als kooperationspolitische Herausforderung der EG, Baden-Baden 1995.

Gerlich, Peter/Glass, Krzysztof : Der schwierige Selbstfindungsprozeß, Vienna 1995.

Glaeßner, Gert-Joachim: Demokratie nach dem Ende des Kommunismus. Regimewechsel, Transition und Demokratisierung im Postkommunismus, Opladen 1995.

Glenny, Misha: Heading off War in the Southern Balcans, in: Foreign Affairs May-June 1995, pp. 98–108.

Gnesotto, Nicole: Lessons of Yugoslavia, WEU Institute for Security Studies, Chaillot Papers March 1994.

Gneveckow, Jürgen: Umweltpolitik in Mittel- und Osteuropa – der Prozeß »Umwelt für Europa«, in: Osteuropa No. 4, 1996, pp. 343–363.

Grabitz, Eberhard (ed.): Abgestufte Integration. Eine Alternative zum herkömmlichen Integrationskonzept, Kehl 1994.

Gros, Daniel/Steinherr, Alfred: Winds of Change. Economic Transition in Central and Eastern Europe, New York 1995.

Halbach, Uwe: Der Islam in der GUS: Die regionale und einzelstaatliche Ebene, in: Berichte des BIOst No. 27, 1996.

Hardi, Peter: Environmental Protection in East-Central Europe. A Market-Oriented Approach, Gütersloh 1994.

Hatschikjan, Magarditsch A./Weilemann, Peter R. (eds.): Nationalismen im Umbruch. Ethnizität, Staat und Politik im neuen Osteuropa, Cologne 1995.

Heckenberger, Wolfgang : Organisierte Kriminalität – Ein Blick in die Welt, in: Kriminalistik No. 4, 1995, pp. 234–239.

Heinrich, Ralph P./Koop, Michael J.: Sozialpolitik im Transformationsprozeß Mittel- und Osteuropas, Tübingen 1996.

Hennig, Ortwin : Die KSZE/OSZE aus deutscher Sicht – Kein Wechsel der Unterstützung, in: Institut für Friedensforschung und Sicherheitspolitik an der Universität Hamburg (ed.): OSZE-Jahrbuch 1995, Baden-Baden 1995, pp. 121–135.

Herrnfeld, Hans-Holger : European by Law. Legal reform and the approximation of law in the Visegrád countries, Gütersloh 1995.

Hickmann, Thorsten: Westliche Wirtschaftskooperation mit Rußland: Tropfen auf den heißen Stein?, in: Osteuropa No. 1, 1995, pp. 30–39.

Hölscher, Jens et al.: Bedingungen ökonomischer Entwicklung in Zentralosteuropa, Vol. 3, Marburg 1995.

Holtbrügge, Dirk: ökonomische Voraussetzungen und Folgen einer Osterweiterung der Europäischen Union, in: Osteuropa No. 6, 1996, pp. 537–547.

Institut für Weltwirtschaft et al. (eds.): Die wirtschaftliche Lage Rußlands. Rußland in der Weltwirtschaft: Noch nicht mehr als ein Exporteur von Rohstoffen. Siebenter Bericht, Teil II. Kieler Diskussionsbeiträge 265, Kiel 1996.

International Commission on the Balkans: Unfinished Peace. Report of the International Commission on the Balkans, Washington 1996.

Jahn, Egbert/Wildenmann, Rudolf (eds.): Stability in East Central Europe? Stabilität in Ostmitteleuropa?, Baden-Baden 1995.

Janning, Josef: Politische und institutionelle Konsequenzen der Erweiterung, in: Weidenfeld, Werner (Hrsg.) Reform der Europäischen Union. Materialien zur Revision des Maastrichter Vertrages 1996, Gütersloh 1995, pp. 265–280.

Janning, Josef: Tendenzen politischer Integration in Europa. Szenarien, Gestaltungsoptionen und Konfliktpotentiale europäischer Politik, in: Nötzold, Jürgen (Hrsg.): Wohin steuert Europa? Erwartungen zu Beginn der 90er Jahre, Baden-Baden 1995, pp. 107–143.

Janning, Josef : Europa braucht verschiedene Geschwindigkeiten, in: Europa-Archiv No. 18, 1994, pp. 527–536.

Janning, Josef : Am Ende der Regierbarkeit? Gefährliche Folgen der Erweiterung der Europäischen Union, in: Europa-Archiv No. 22, 1993, pp. 645–652.

Janning, Josef/Algieri, Franco: The German Debate, in: The 1996 IGC – National Debates (2): Germany, Spain, Sweden and the UK, Discussion Paper 67, The Royal Institute of International Affairs, London 1996, pp. 1–21.

Janning, Josef/Ochmann, Cornelius: Beyond Europhoria. Political and Economic Relations between East and West in Europe, in: Ehrhart, Hans-Georg et al. (eds.): The Former Soviet Union and European Security: Between Integration and Re-Nationalization, Baden-Baden 1993, pp. 147–165.

Jennewein, Marga: Finanztransfer und Finanzhilfe für Osteuropa, in: ifo Schnelldienst No. 31, 1995, pp. 27–33.

Jung, Christian: Die Osterweiterung und die Interessen der EU-

Mitglieder, in: Wirtschaftspolitische Blätter No. 3–4, 1995, pp. 246–253.

Kaiser, Karl/Brüning, Martin (eds.): East-Central Europe and the EU: Problems of Integration, Bonn 1996.

Kaiser, Karl: Umgestaltung der NATO, in: Internationale Politik No. 6, 1996, pp. 35–46.

Klebes, Heinrich: Menschenrechte, Minderheitenschutz: Markenzeichen des Europarats, in: Antretter, Robert (ed.): Quo vadis Europarat?, Bonn 1995, pp. 16–21.

Kortunov, Andrej: Zwischen Imperium und Weltharmonie, in: Internationale Politik No. 1 1997, pp. 9–14.

Kühnhardt, Ludger: Die NATO im Prozeß der inneren und äußeren Veränderung, in: Aus Politik und Zeitgeschichte No. B5, 1996, pp. 12–20.

Lambsdorff, Otto Graf/Karaganov, Sergei A.: Russia's Economic Role in Europe. Report of the Commission for the Greater Europe, Vol. II, Vienna 1995.

Lippert, Barbara/Schneider, Heinrich (eds.): Monitoring Association and Beyond: The European Union and the Visegrád States, Bonn 1995.

Ludlow, Peter et al.: Preparing for Membership. The Eastward and Southern Enlargement of the EU, Brussels 1996.

Lutz, Dieter S.: Die OSZE im Übergang von der Sicherheitsarchitektur des Zwanzigsten Jahrhunderts zum Sicherheitsmodell des Einundzwanzigsten Jahrhunderts, in: Institut für Friedensforschung und Sicherheitspolitik an der Universität Hamburg (ed.): OSZE-Jahrbuch 1995, Baden-Baden 1995, pp. 63–96.

Mangott, Gerhard: East European Reform Countries: Problems of Democratic Consolidation and External Relations, Laxenburg 1996.

Markotich, Stan/Moy, Patricia: Political Attitudes in Serbia, in: RFE/RL Research Report 15 April 1994.

Martin, Laurence/Roper John (eds.): Towards a Common Defence Policy. A Study by the European Strategy Group and the Institute for Security Studies of Western European Union, Paris 1995.

Maurer, Andreas/Thiele, Burkhard (eds.): Legitimationsprobleme und Demokratisierung der Europäischen Union, Marburg 1996.

Meier, Christian: Wirtschaftsbeziehungen zwischen den Staaten Osteuropas: Regionale Kooperation auf dem Prüfstand, in: Berichte des BIOst No. 36, 1995.

Meissner, Boris/Eisfeld, Alfred (eds.): Die GUS-Staaten in Europa und Asien, Baden-Baden 1995.

National Defense Research Institute (ed.): Enlarging NATO. The Russia Factor, Santa Monica 1996.

Neuhold, Hanspeter et al.: Political and Economic Transformation in East Central Europe, Boulder 1995.

Österreichisches Institut für Wirtschaftsforschung (ed.): Report – The Economies of Central and Eastern Europe, Recent Trends and Prospects for 1996, Vienna 1996.

Oeter, Stefan: Bosnien und Europa – ein Unfall der Völkerrechtsordnung?, in: Nenad, Stefanov/Werz, Michael (eds.): Bosnien und Europa. Die Ethnisierung der Gesellschaft, Frankfurt/M. 1995.

Olt, Reinhard (ed.): Der Riese erwacht. Osteuropa nach 1989. Facetten aus Gesellschaft, Politik und Medien, Frankfurt/M. 1995.

Oschlies, Wolf: Ex-Jugoslawien '95. Politisch-ökonomische Portraits der sechs Nachfolgestaaten, in: Berichte des BIOst No. 54, 1995.

Perry, Duncan M.: On the Road to Stability – or Destruction?, in: Transition 25 August 1995.

Przeworski, Adam et al.: Sustainable Democracy, Cambridge 1995.

Quaisser, Wolfgang: Der Außenhandel Mittel- und Osteuropas im Lichte der Osterweiterung der Europäischen Union, Working Paper No. 187, Munich 1995.

Rahr, Alexander: Die Sicherung der Energietransportwege. Eine strategische Aufgabe für Rußland, in: Internationale Politik No. 1 1997, pp. 25–30

Rahr, Alexander/Krause, Joachim: Russia's New Foreign Policy, in: Deutsche Gesellschaft für Auswärtige Politik (ed.): Arbeitspapiere zur Internationalen Politik No. 91, 1995.

Reuter, Jens: Die Wirtschaft der BR Jugoslawien nach der Suspendierung der Sanktionen, in: Südosteuropa, Vol. 45 8/1996.

Reuter, Jürgen: Athens schwieriger Weg zum Abschluß eines Interim-Abkommens mit Skopje, in: Südosteuropa-Mitteilungen Vol. 35 No. 4, 1995, pp. 333–359.

Rieff, David: Slaughterhouse. Bosnia and the Failure of the West, New York 1995.

Rose, Richard: Mobilizing demobilized voters in post-communist Societies, in: Party Politics No. 4, 1995, pp. 549–563.

Rubin, Barnett R. (ed.): Towards Comprehensive Peace in Southeast Europe. Conflict Prevention in the South Balkans, New York 1996.

Rudka, Andrzej/Mizsei, Kálmán: East Central Europe Between Disintegration and Reintegration. Is CEFTA the Solution?, New York 1995.

Rudolph, Hedwig (ed.): Geplanter Wandel, ungeplante Wirkungen, Berlin 1995.

Rupnik, Jacques et al.: Challenges in the East, The Hague 1995.

Santel, Bernhard: Migration in und nach Europa. Erfahrungen. Strukturen. Politik, Opladen 1995.

Schilling, Walter: Rußlands Politik der Nonproliferation, in: Osteuropa No. 8, 1995, pp. 709–716.

Schmidt, Fabian: The Sandzak: Muslims between Serbia and Montenegro, in: RFE/RL Research Report 11 February 1994.

Seewann, Gerhard (ed.): Minderheiten als Konfliktpotential in Ostmittel- und Südosteuropa, Munich 1995.

Segbers, Klaus/De Spiegeleire, Stephan (eds.): Post-Soviet Puzzles. Mapping the Political Economy of the Former Soviet Union, in: Stiftung Wissenschaft und Politik (ed.): Aktuelle Materialien zur Internationalen Politik, Vol. 40, Baden-Baden 1995.

Segert, Dieter et al.: Parteien in Osteuropa. Kontext und Akteure, Opladen 1995.

SINUS Moscow: Russische Außenpolitik 1996 im Urteil von außenpolitischen Experten, Befragung des SINUS-Instituts im Auftrag der Friedrich-Ebert-Stiftung, Moscow Office 1996.

SINUS Moscow: Die Kommunikationsélite in Rußland 1995, Befragung des SINUS-Instituts im Auftrag der Friedrich-Ebert-Stiftung, Moscow Office 1996.

Spanger, Hans-Joachim/Kokeev, Aleksandr: Brücken, Achsen – und neue Gräben. Die deutsch-russischen Beziehungen im multilateralen Spannungsfeld, in: Hessische Stiftung Friedens- und Konfliktforschung (ed.): HFSK-Report No. 6, 1995, Frankfurt/M. 1995.

Stanners David/Bourdeau, Philippe (eds.): Europe's Environment. The Dob?í

Steffani, Winfried/Thaysen, Uwe (eds.): Demokratie in Europa: Zur Rolle der Parlamente, Opladen 1995.

Stehn, Jürgen: Stufen einer Osterweiterung der Europäischen Union, in: Die Weltwirtschaft No. 2, 1994, pp. 194–219.

Stiftung Wissenschaft und Politik (ed.): Westliche Wirtschaftshilfe für Rußland, Aktuelle SWP-Dokumentation No. 15, Ebenhausen 1995.

Sundhausen, Holm: Experiment Jugoslawien. Von der Staatsgründung bis zum Zerfall, Mannheim 1993.

Swerew, Jurij M.: Rußlands Gebiet Kaliningrad im neuen geopolitischen Koordinatenfeld, in: Berichte des BIOst No. 6, 1996.

Szelényi, Iván/Szelényi, Szonja: Circulation or Reproduction of Élites during the Post-Communist Transformation in Eastern Europe, in: Theory and Society Vol. 24, 1995, pp. 615–638.

Tangermann, Stefan: Osterweiterung der EU: Wird die Agrarpolitik zum Hindernis?, in: Wirtschaftsdienst No. 9, 1995, pp. 484–491.

Taroor, Shashi: The Role of the United Nations in European Peacekeeping, in: Chayes, Abram/Handler Chayes, Antonia (eds.): Preventing Conflict in the Post-Communist World. Mobilizing International and Regional Organizations, Washington 1996, pp. 467–482.

Timmermann, Heinz: Die Europäische Union und Rußland – Dimensionen und Perspektiven der Partnerschaft, in: Integration No. 4 1996, pp. 195–207.

Timmermann, Heinz: Die Gemeinschaft Unabhängiger Staaten: Konvergenzen und Divergenzen, in: Aktuelle Analysen des BIOst No. 58, 1995.

Timmermann, Heinz: Rußlands Außenpolitik: Die Europäische Dimension, in: Osteuropa No. 6, 1995, pp. 495–508.

Timmermann, Heinz: Rußland und Deutschland. Ihre Beziehungen als integraler Bestandteil gesamteuropäischer Integration, in: Berichte des BIOst No. 39, 1995.

Troebst, Stefan: Macedonia – Powder Keg Defused?, in: RFE/RL Research Report 28 January 1994.

UN-Economic Commission for Europe: Economic Bulletin for Europe Vol. 47, New York 1995.

Vienna Institute for Comparative Economic Studies (ed.): The Countries in Transition 1995, WIIW Handbook of Statistics, Vienna 1995.

Vincentz, Volker: Auswirkungen der wachsenden Arbeitsteilung zwischen Deutschland und seinen östlichen Nachbarn auf Arbeitsmarkt, Investitionen und Güterströme, Working Papers No. 188, Munich December 1995.

Vogel, Heinrich (ed.): Rußland als Partner in der europäischen Politik, in: Berichte des BIOst No. 8, 1996.

Weber, Ralf L.: Außenwirtschaft und Systemtransformation: Zur Bedeutung der Zahlungsbilanzrestriktionen im Übergang von der Zentralplanwirtschaft zur Marktwirtschaft, Stuttgart 1995.

Weidenfeld, Werner (ed.): Demokratie und Marktwirtschaft in Osteuropa, Gütersloh 1996.

Weidenfeld, Werner (ed.) Reform der Europäischen Union. Materialien zur Revision des Maastrichter Vertrages 1996, Gütersloh 1995.

Weidenfeld, Werner (ed.): Europe '96. Reforming the European Union, Gütersloh 1994.

Weidenfeld, Werner (ed.): Central and Eastern Europe on the Way into the European Union, Gütersloh 1994 ff.

Weidenfeld, Werner/Janning, Josef: Europe: What Needs to be Done. Strategy Paper for the International Bertelsmann Forum, in: Bertelsmann Foundation Publishers (eds.): Europe's Political Agenda for the Nineties, Gütersloh 1995, pp. 151–175.

Weidenfeld, Werner/Janning, Josef: The new Europe. Strategies of differentiated Integration. Presentation for the International Bertelsmann Forum on the Petersberg on 19–20 January 1996.

Weißenburger, Ulrich: Sicherheitsmängel und Störfallrisiken als Problem der russischen Wirtschafts- und Umweltpolitik, Teil I: Umweltgefährdung durch Sicherheitsdefizite im nichtnuklearen Bereich, in: Berichte des BIOst No. 14, 1996.

Weißenburger, Ulrich: Sicherheitsmängel und Störfallrisiken als Problem der russischen Wirtschafts- und Umweltpolitik, Teil II: Umweltgefährdung durch Nuklearanlagen und radioaktive Abfälle, in: Berichte des BIOst No. 15, 1996.

Welfens, Paul J. J.: Die Europäische Union und die mittelosteuropäischen Länder. Entwicklungen, Probleme, politische Optionen, in: Berichte des BIOst No. 7, 1995.

WeltTrends (ed.): NATO-Osterweiterung. Neue Mitglieder für ein altes Bündnis?, Berlin 1996.

Woodard, Colin: Buildung Up Bosnia's Army, in: Transition 1 November 1996.

World Bank: Bosnia and Herzegovina. Toward Economic Recovery, Washington 1996.

World Bank: World Development Report, Washington 1996.

Zagorski, Andrei: Die Entwicklungstendenzen in der GUS. Von der Differenzierung zur Konsolidierung, in: Berichte des BIOst No. 24, 1994.

Zagorski, Andrei: Die neuen »Unionen« in der GUS: Ernsthaft und auf Dauer?, in: Aktuelle Analysen des BIOst No. 38, 1996.

Zumach, Andreas: Weltpolitische Agonie, Großmächte zwischen Ohnmacht und Kollaboration, in: Lettre International No. 31 1995, pp. 104–105.

The authors

Eric von Breska
Research Fellow of the Research Group on European Affairs at the Center for Applied Policy Research of the Ludwig-Maximilians-University of Munich; born on 4 January 1969 in Offenbach; studies of political science, economics, modern history and Slavic languages and literature in Munich; 1991 studies at the State University of Linguistics in Moscow; 1992 practical training with the Transnational Corporations and Management Division of the Department of Economic and Social Development of the United Nations in New York; 1993 practical training with the Academic Service of the German Bundestag; 1994 M.A. graduation from the University of Munich; 1995/96 staff member of the Department "International Economic Relations East Central Europe and Successor States of the Soviet Union" at the Stiftung Wissenschaft und Politik in Ebenhausen; since 1996 Research Fellow of the Research Group on European Affairs.

Publications include: Doppelherrschaft und Verfassungskrieg in Rußland; in: Mommsen, Margareta (ed.): Demokratie-Experimente im Postkommunismus. Politischer und institutioneller Wandel in Osteuropa, Münster 1995, pp. 49–76; Ein größeres Europa – Die EU bereitet die Erweiterung vor, Europäische Kommission (ed.), Brussels 1997.

Petra Brunner
Research Fellow of the Research Group on European Affairs at the Center for Applied Policy Research of the Ludwig-Maximilians-Univer-

sity of Munich; born on 25 July 1965 in Munich; studies of political science, economics and international relations in Munich and Paris; 1991 diploma at the Hochschule für Politik (Academy of Political Sciences) in Munich; 1988–1991 lecturer for Eastern European instructors at the Goethe Institute in Munich and Berlin; 1991/92 scholarship holder of the Council of the European Movement at the College of Europe/Brugge (Belgium); 1992 Diplôme de Hautes Études Européennes at the College of Europe; 1992/93 trainee with the European Commission in Brussels; 1993–1995 Research Fellow of the ifo Institut für Wirtschaftsforschung in Munich; since 1995 Research Fellow of the Research Group on European Affairs.

Publications include: Auswirkungen der zunehmenden Liberalisierung des Welthandels und der Internationalisierung des Arbeitsmarktes (co-author), Munich 1995; in: ifo Schnelldienst: Subsidiarität – Leerformel oder Orientierungshilfe zur Kompetenzverteilung in der EG? No. 22 1993, pp. 7–13; Die politischen und wirtschaftlichen Beziehungen der EU zu den Visegrádstaaten, No. 14 1994, pp. 14–22; Außenwirtschaftsbeziehungen EU-Japan: Kooperation statt Konfrontation (with E. Chenot), No. 15 1995, pp. 3–9; Die Europäische Union zwischen Vertiefung und Erweiterung (with W. Ochel), No. 3 1995, pp. 9–20.

Martin Brusis, PhD

Research Fellow of the Research Group on European Affairs at the Center for Applied Policy Research of the Ludwig-Maximilians-University of Munich; born on 10 June 1965 in Soest. Studies of political science and Slavic languages and literature in Marburg and Berlin; 1991 diploma at the Department of Political Science of the Free University of Berlin; 1992–1994 participation in a research project on "Symbolic-integrative mobilisation strategies of new political actors in Poland, Hungary and the Czech Republic" at the Institute for Eastern European Studies of the Free University; 1995 doctorate in sociology with a political field analysis on the Hungarian privatisation policy; since 1995 Research Fellow at the Research Group of European Affairs.

Publications include: Privatisierungspolitik in Ungarn, Polen und der Tschechoslowakei. Überlegungen zu einer vergleichenden Analyse, in: Osteuropa, No. 7–8 1993, pp. 687–686; Korporatismus als Transformationskonsens. Der Fall Ungarn im osteuropäischen Vergleich, in: Initial. Berliner Debatte, No. 3/4 1994, pp. 25–35; Entstehungsbedingungen der Arbeitslosenversicherung in Ungarn, in: Zeitschrift für ausländisches und internationales Arbeits- und Sozialrecht, No. 3 1995, pp. 336–368; Systemtransformation als Entscheidungsprozeß. Eine Politikfeldanalyse zur Privatisierung in Ungarn, Berlin 1995.

Josef Janning
Director of the Research Group on European Affairs at the Center for Applied Policy Research of the Ludwig-Maximilians-University of Munich; deputy director of the Center for Applied Policy Research; born on 2 May 1956 in Bocholt; studies of political science, modern history and German language and literature at the universities of Bonn, Cologne and Elmira College, N.Y., USA (B.A., Political Science); 1985 M.A. graduation (political science) with a paper "On the image of the USA in the peace movements of the Federal Republic of Germany 1979–1984"; 1982–1985 lecturer in political science for American scholarship holders at the Academic Foreign Exchange Department of the University of Bonn; 1985–1987 research fellow at the Institute for Political Science of the University of Mainz, International Politics Department; 1987/88 lecturer in Political Science, 1987–1995 deputy head of the Research Group on European Affairs at the Institute for Political Science of the University of Mainz; since 1995 director of the Research Group on European Affairs at the Center for Applied Policy Research of the Ludwig-Maximilians-University of Munich.

Publications include: Beyond Europhoria. Political and Economic Relations between East and West in Europe (with C. Ochmann), in: Ehrhart, Hans-Georg et al. (eds.): The Former Soviet Union and European Security: Between Integration and Re-Nationalization, Baden-Baden 1993, pp. 147–165; Am Ende der Regierbarkeit? Gefährliche Folgen der Erweiterung der Europäischen Union, in: Europa-Archiv, 22 1993, pp. 645–652; Europa braucht verschiedene Geschwindigkeiten, in: Europa-Archiv, 18 1994, pp. 527–536; Politische und institutionelle Konsequenzen der Erweiterung, in: Weidenfeld, Werner (ed.): Reform der Europäischen Union, Materialien zur Revision des Maastrichter Vertrages 1996, Gütersloh 1995, pp. 265–280; Tendenzen politischer Integration in Europa. Szenarien, Gestaltungsoptionen und Konfliktpotentiale europäischer Politik, in: Nötzold, Jürgen (ed.): Wohin steuert Europa? Erwartungen zu Beginn der 90er Jahre, Baden-Baden 1995, pp. 107–143; Europe: What Needs to be Done. Strategy Paper for the International Bertelsmann Forum (with Werner Weidenfeld), in: Bertelsmann Foundation Publishers (eds.): Europe's Political Agenda for the Nineties, Gütersloh 1995, pp. 151–175; A German Europe – a European Germany? On the debate over Germany's foreign policy, in: International Affairs, Vol. 72, No. 1, 1996, pp. 33–41; The German Debate, in: The 1996 IGC – National Debates (2): Germany, Spain, Sweden and the UK (with F. Algieri), Discussion Paper 67, The Royal Institute of International Affairs, London 1996, pp. 1–21; Zur Reform des Abstimmungsverfahrens im Rat der Europäischen Union: Überlegungen und Modellrechnungen (with C. Deubner), in: Integration No. 3 1996, pp. 146–158; Europäische Integration, in: Weidenfeld, Werner/Korte, Karl-Rudolf (eds.): Handbuch zur deutschen Einheit, Neuausgabe Frankfurt 1996, pp. 275–283.

Barbara von Ow
Research Fellow of the Research Group on European Affairs at the Center for Applied Policy Research of the Ludwig-Maximilians-University of Munich; born on 19 April 1957 in Munich; studies of German and French language and literature at the universities of Munich and Oxford; 1980–1983 correspondent of Reuters News Agency in Vienna and London; 1984–1986 expert on German policy in the Reseach Department of Radio Free Europe in Munich; 1989–1990 member of the Advisory Board of the Daedalus journal of the American Academy of Arts and Sciences (Eastern Europe ... Central Europe ... Europe); 1987–1989 foreign policy editor of the Süddeutsche Zeitung, mainly on Eastern European issues; 1990–1992 freelancer of the Süddeutsche Zeitung in Paris; member of the editorial committee of the European journal Belvédère; 1992–1994 freelance correspondent of the Süddeutsche Zeitung in Moscow; since 1995 research fellow of the Research Group on European Affairs.

Publications include: numerous journalist publications, mainly on Eastern Europe and Russia; Das Recht, in die Welt einzugreifen, in: Václav Havel – Friedenspreisträger 1989, Börsenblatt für den Deutschen

Buchhandel, Vol. 45, 11 September 1989; L'Allemagne, l'Europe et la France, interview with Harry Maier in: Politique Etrangère 1/1990, pp. 99–118; The accession of the countries of Central and Eastern Europe into the European Union: problems and perspectives, in: Weidenfeld, Werner (ed.): Central and Eastern Europe on the Way into the European Union, Gütersloh 1995, pp. 267–279; Polen, Slowakei, Tschechien, Ungarn, in: Weidenfeld, Werner/Wessels, Wolfgang (eds.): Jahrbuch der Europäischen Integration 1995/1996.

Professor Dr. Dr. h.c. Werner Weidenfeld
born 1947 in Cohem/Moselle; studies of political science, history and philosophy; 1971 doctorate; 1975 habilitation (post-doctorate); 1975–1995 professor in political science at the University of Mainz; 1986–1988 guest professor at the Sorbonne, Paris; since 1995 professor in political science at the Ludwig-Maximilians-University of Munich; Director of the Center for Applied Policy Research in Munich; since 1987 coordinator for German-American cooperation of the Federal Government; editor of the journal "Internationale Politik"; member of the board of the Bertelsmann Foundation.

Publications include: Global Responsibilities. Europe in Tomorrow's World. Basic Findings 7, Gütersloh 1991, 2nd edition 1993 (co-editor with Josef Janning); Europe in Global Change, Gütersloh 1993 (co-editor with Josef Janning); Eastern Europe: Challenges - Problems - Strategies. Working Papers 8, Gütersloh 1993 (with Manfred Huterer); Internal Security and the Single Market, Gütersloh 1994 (with Reinhard Rupprecht and Markus Hellenthal); Europe '96. Reforming the European Union, Gütersloh 1994 (editor); Europe and the Middle East (Gütersloh 1995); Central and Eastern Europe on the Way into the European Union. Problems and Prospects of Integration, Gütersloh 1996 (editor); Transformation in the Middle East and North Africa, Gütersloh 1996 (with Josef Janning and Sven Behrendt); America and Europe: Is the Break Inevitable?, Gütersloh 1996; Europa von A–Z. Taschenbuch der europäischen Integration (co-editor with Wolfgang Wessels); Jahrbuch der Europäischen Integration (co-editor with Wolfgang Wessels).

The project partners

Bertelsmann Science Foundation

In line with the aims and duties set out in its statute, the Bertelsmann Science Foundation sees itself as an institution focusing on, inter alia, improving European and global cooperation and integration, and the competent organisation of international cooperation in the fields of security, economy, politics, culture and ecology.

This is also the objective with which it has, since July 1995, continued the project "Strategies for Europe", originally initiated by the Bertelsmann Foundation. By providing concepts, contents and material, the project is to contribute to the solution of present and future European policy problems. At the same time it is to improve understanding between the European countries and intensify European integration, while maintaining national and regional cultural identity. In order to provide conceptual support for this scheme, the Bertelsmann Science Foundation has set up an international strategy group, which consists of high-ranking experts from the political, economic and scientific spheres. Results are published, e. g. in the "Strategies for Europe" publication series.

Research Group on European Affairs

The Research Group on European Affairs at the Center for Applied Policy Research of the Ludwig-Maximilians-University of Munich is responsible for providing scientific assistance in developing and implementing the project objectives and transferring information. The Research Group on European Affairs can look back on many years of wide-ranging experience in the intensive research into European questions. Numerous publications on European unification and cooperation in the "Jahrbuch der Europäischen Integration" give proof of this work. In addition, the Research Group on European Affairs has comprehensive research facilities at its disposal. Apart from two editorial teams these include a research library and the European Documentation Center, which has access to all documents and publications issued by the executive bodies of the European Union and is linked to the European data network.

The publications

As a direct outcome of the work on the project "Strategies for Europe" the publications listed in the following have so far been issued:

Information on the approach, the objectives, the fields of work:

Bertelsmann Stiftung (ed.), *Strategien und Optionen für die Zukunft Europas. Ziele und Konturen eines Projektes.* Gütersloh 1988. 24 p. Free of charge.

Bertelsmann Foundation (ed.), *Strategies and Options for the Future of Europe. Aims and Contours of a Project.* Gütersloh 1989. 24 p. Free of charge.

Fondation Bertelsmann (ed.), *Stratégies et options pour l'avenir de l'Europe. Objectifs et countours d'un projet.* Gütersloh 1989. 24 p. Free of charge.

Fondazione Bertelsmann (ed.), *Strategie e opzioni per il futuro dell'Europa. Obiettivi e contorni di un progetto.* Gütersloh 1988. 22 p. Free of charge.

Bertelsmann Stiftung, *Ziele und Voraussetzungen eines geeinten Europas.* Vorstellung des Projektes "Strategien und Optionen für die Zukunft Europas". Mit Beiträgen von Valentin M. Falin, Henry A. Kissinger, Reinhard Mohn, Werner Weidenfeld. Gütersloh 1988. 44 p. Free of charge.

Werner Weidenfeld, Hermann Lübbe, Werner Maihofer, Joseph Rovan,

Europäische Kultur: das Zukunftsgut des Kontinents. Vorschläge für eine europäische Kulturpolitik. Gütersloh 1990. 124 p. Free of charge.

Werner Weidenfeld et al., *Herausforderung Mittelmeer – die europäische Antwort. Aufgaben, Ziele und Instrumente einer europäischen Politik.* Gütersloh 1991. 40 p. Free of charge.

In the series "Basic Findings":

Forschungsgruppe Europa, *Europäische Defizite, europäische Perspektiven – eine Bestandsaufnahme für morgen.* Grundlagen 1. Gütersloh 1988. 222 p., ISBN 3-89204-011-7. DM 20.00.

Research Group on European Affairs, *European Deficits, European Perspectives – Taking Stock for Tomorrow.* Basic Findings 1. Gütersloh 1989. 232 p., ISBN 3-89204-018-4. DM 20.00.

Rolf H. Hasse, *The European Central Bank: Perspectives for a Future Development of the European Monetary System.* Basic Findings 2. Gütersloh 1990. 280 p., ISBN 3-89204-036-2. DM 20.00.

Wolfgang Däubler, *Sozialstaat EG? Die andere Dimension des Binnenmarktes.* Grundlagen 3. Gütersloh 1989. 208 p., ISBN 3-89204-026-5. DM 20.00.

Wolfgang Däubler, *Market and Social Justice in the EC – the Other Dimension of the Internal Market.* Basic Findings 3. Gütersloh 1991. 216 p., ISBN 3-89204-041-9. DM 20.00.

Dieter Biehl, Horst Winter, *Europa finanzieren – ein föderalistisches Modell.* Grundlagen 4. Gütersloh 1990. 176 p., ISBN 3-89204-028-1. DM 20.00.

Bertelsmann Stiftung (ed.), *Die Zukunft Europas – Kultur und Verfassung des Kontinents.* Grundlagen 5. Gütersloh 1991. 334 p., ISBN 3-89204-048-6. DM 20.00.

Lutz Wicke, Burkhard Huckestein, *Umwelt Europa – der Ausbau zur ökologischen Marktwirtschaft.* Grundlagen 6. Gütersloh 1991. 256 p., ISBN 3-89204-049-4. DM 20.00.

Werner Weidenfeld, Josef Janning (eds.), *Global Responsibilities: Europe in Tomorrow's World.* Basic Findings 7. Gütersloh 1991. 2nd edition 1993. 240 p., ISBN 3-89204-053-2. DM 20.00.

Kenneth Button, *Europäische Verkehrspolitik – Wege in die Zukunft.* Grundlagen 8. Gütersloh 1992. 192 p., ISBN 3-89204-055-9. DM 20.00.

Kenneth Button, *Transport Policy – Ways into Europe's Future. Basic Findings* 8. Gütersloh 1994. 228 p., ISBN 3-89204-065-6. DM 20.00.

Klaus W. Grewlich, *Europa im globalen Technologiewettlauf: Der Weltmarkt wird zum Binnenmarkt.* Grundlagen 9. Gütersloh 1992. 352 p., ISBN 3-89204-054-0. DM 20.00.

Reinhard Rupprecht, Markus Hellenthal, *Innere Sicherheit im Europäischen Binnenmarkt.* Grundlagen 10. Gütersloh 1992. 392 p., ISBN 3-89204-058-3. DM 20.00.

Reinhard Rupprecht, Markus Hellenthal, Werner Weidenfeld. *Internal Security and the Single Market.* Gütersloh 1994. 62 p., ISBN 3-89204-140-7. DM 12.00.

Werner Weidenfeld (ed.), *Herausforderung Mittelmeer: Aufgaben, Ziele und Strategien europäischer Politik.* Grundlagen 11. Gütersloh 1992. 244 p., ISBN 3-89204-063-X. DM 20.00.

In the series "Working Papers":

Forschungsgruppe Europa (ed.), *Binnenmarkt '92: Perspektiven aus deutscher Sicht.* Arbeitspapiere 1. Gütersloh 1988. 4th edition 1989. 224 p., ISBN 3-89204-015-X. DM 12.00.

Werner Weidenfeld, Walther Stützle, Curt Gasteyger, Josef Janning, *Die Architekur europäischer Sicherheit: Probleme, Kriterien, Perspektiven.* Arbeitspapiere 2. Gütersloh 1989. 74 p., ISBN 3-89204-020-6. DM 12.00.

Bertelsmann Stiftung (ed.), *Die Vollendung des Europäischen Währungssystems.* Arbeitspapiere 3. Gütersloh 1989. 72 p., ISBN 3-89204-024-9. DM 12.00.

Werner Weidenfeld, Josef Janning, *Der Umbruch Europas: die Zukunft des Kontinents.* Arbeitspapiere 4. Gütersloh 1990. 72 p., ISBN 3-89204-032-X. DM 12.00.

Werner Weidenfeld, Christine Holeschovsky, Elmar Brok, Fritz Franzmeier, Dieter Schumacher, Jürgen Klose, *Die doppelte Integration:*

Europa und das größere Deutschland. Arbeitspapiere 6. Gütersloh 1991. 108 p., ISBN 3-89204-042-7. DM 12.00.

Werner Weidenfeld, *Wie Europa verfaßt sein soll. Materialien zur Politischen Union.* Arbeitspapiere 7. Gütersloh 1991. 456 p., ISBN 3-89204-045-1. DM 12.00.

Werner Weidenfeld (ed.), *Der vollendete Binnenmarkt – eine Herausforderung für die Europäische Gemeinschaft.* Arbeitspapiere 11. Gütersloh 1993. 152 p., ISBN 3-89204-072-9. DM 12.00.

Further Publications:

Werner Weidenfeld (ed.), *Demokratie und Marktwirtschaft in Osteuropa.* Revised and updated version. Gütersloh 1995. 584 p., ISBN 3-89204-166-0. DM 48.00.

Werner Weidenfeld, Josef Janning (eds.), *Europe in Global Change.* Gütersloh 1993. 288 p., ISBN 3-89204-084-2. DM 34.00. 2nd edition.

Sergei A. Karaganov, *Whither Western Aid to Russia. A Russian View of Western Support.* Gütersloh 1994. 92 p., ISBN 3-89204-132-6. DM 15.00.

Grigorij Jawlinskij, *Reform von unten – Die neue Zukunft Rußlands.* Gütersloh 1994. 192 p., ISBN 3-89204-119-9. DM 25.00.

Werner Weidenfeld (ed.), *Das europäische Einwanderungskonzept.* Gütersloh 1994. 200 p., ISBN 3-89204-088-5. DM 25.00.

Werner Weidenfeld (ed.), *Maastricht in der Analyse. Materialien zur Europäischen Union.* Gütersloh 1994. 502 p., ISBN 3-89204-111-3. DM 25.00.

Werner Weidenfeld (ed.), *Europa '96. Reforming the European Union.* Gütersloh 1994. 60 p., ISBN 3-89204-154-7. Also in German ISBN 3-89204-151-2 (DM 10.00), French ISBN 3-89204-155-5, and Italian ISBN 3-89204-170-9. Free of charge. Spanish version out of print.

Peter Hardi, *Environmental Protection in East-Central Europe: A Market-Oriented Approach.* Gütersloh 1994. 136 p., ISBN 3-89204-137-7. DM 15.00.

Bertelsmann Foundation (ed.), *Central and Eastern Europe and the Eu-*

ropean Union. Problems and Prospects of Integration. Gütersloh 1995. 172 p., ISBN 3-89204-164-4. Also in German. ISBN 3-89204-163-6. Free of charge.

Werner Weidenfeld (ed.), *Reform der Europäischen Union. Materialien zu Revision des Maastrichter Vertrages 1996.* Gütersloh 1995. 426 p., ISBN 3-89204-127-X. DM 20.00.

William R. Smyser, *The Europe of Berlin. On a New Division of Labor Across the Atlantic.* Gütersloh 1995. 48 p., ISBN 3-89204-182-2. DM 15.00.

Werner Weidenfeld (ed.), *Europe and the Middle East.* Gütersloh 1995. 60 p., ISBN 3-89204-183-0. Also in German ISBN 3-89204-204-7 and Arabic ISBN 3-89204-210-1. DM 12.00.

Werner Weidenfeld, Jürgen Turek, *Standort Europa. Handeln in der neuen Weltwirtschaft.* Gütersloh 1995. 230 p., ISBN 3-89204-177-6. DM 25.00.

Miles Kahler, Werner Link, *Europa und Amerika nach der Zeitenwende – die Wiederkehr der Geschichte.* Gütersloh 1995. 176 p., ISBN 3-89204-148-2. DM 20.00.

Joseph Rovan, *Europa und die Welt von morgen.* Gütersloh 1995. 52 p., ISBN 3-89204-178-4. DM 15.00.

Hans-Holger Herrnfeld, *Recht europäisch. Rechtsreform und Rechtsangleichung in den Visegrád-Staaten.* Gütersloh 1995. 182 p., ISBN 3-89204-212-8. DM 25.00.

Werner Weidenfeld (ed.), *Mittel- und Osteuropa auf dem Weg in die Europäische Union. Bericht zum Stand der Integrationsfähigkeit.* Gütersloh 1995. 288 p., ISBN 3-89204-214-4.

Bertelsmann Stiftung (ed.), *Europe's Political Agenda for the Nineties. International Bertelmann Forum.* Gütersloh 1996. 176 p., ISBN 3-89204-136-9. Also in German ISBN 3-89204-135-0. DM 20.00.

Wolfgang H. Reinicke, *Deepening the Atlantic. Toward a New Transatlantic Marketplace?* Gütersloh 1996. 96 p., ISBN 3-89204-802-9. DM 18.00.

Curt Gasteyger, *An Ambiguous Power. The European Union in an Changeing World.* Gütersloh 1996. 160 p., ISBN 3-89204-807-X. DM 20.00.

Heinz Laufer, Thomas Fischer, *Föderalismus als Strukturprinzip für die*

Europäische Union. Gütersloh 1996. 196 p., ISBN 3-89204-801-0. DM 20.00.

Wolfgang Reinicke, *Tugging at the Sleeves of Politicans.* Think Tanks – American Experiences and German Perspectives. Gütersloh 1996. 72 p., ISBN 3-89204-236-5. Also in German ISBN 3-89204-235-7. DM 12.00.

Georg Brunner, *Nationality Problems and Minority Conflicts in Eastern Europe.* Updated and completely revised edition. Gütersloh 1996, 198 p. ISBN 3-89204-808-8. Also in German ISBN 3-89204-800-2. DM 25.00.

Werner Weidenfeld, *America and Europe: Is the Break Inevitable?* Gütersloh 1996. 152 p., ISBN 3-89204-249-7. Also in German ISBN 3-89204-228-4. DM 32.00.

Franco Algieri, Josef Janning, Dirk Rumberg (eds.), *Managing Security in Europe. The European Union and the challenge of enlargement.* Gütersloh 1996. 272 p., ISBN 3-89204-805-3. DM 30.00.

Josef Janning, Dirk Rumberg (eds.), *Peace and Stability in the Middle East and North Africa.* Gütersloh 1996. 142 p., ISBN 3-89204-243-8. DM 20.00.

Max Kaase, Andrew Kohut, *Estranged Friends?* The Transatlantic Consequences of Societal Change. Gütersloh 1996. 152 p., ISBN 3-89204-149-0. DM 15.00.

Stefan Collignon, *Geldwertstabilität für Europa.* Die Währungsunion auf dem Prüfstand. Gütersloh 1996. 200 p. ISBN 3-89204-811-8. DM 25.00.

Werner Weidenfeld (ed.), *Transformation in the Middle East and North Africa.* Challenges and Potentials for Europe and its Partners. Gütersloh 1997. 60 p., ISBN 3-89204-278-0. Also in German ISBN 3-89204-277-2. DM 15.00.

Werner Weidenfeld (ed.), *Neue Ostpolitik.* Strategie für eine gesamteuropäische Entwicklung. Gütersloh 1997. 192 p., ISBN 3-89204-810-X. DM 20.00.

Werner Weidenfeld (ed.), *Central and Eastern Europe on the Way into the European Union.* Problems and Prospects of Integration in 1996. Gütersloh 1997. 270 p., ISBN 3-89204-812-6. Also in German ISBN 3-89204-809-6. DM 15.00.